GEOGRAPHY I

The Middle East, North Africa, & Europe

Teacher Guide

Laura Bateman and Brett Vaden

MEMORIA PRESS

Teaching Guidelines

One goal of this course is to familiarize students with the countries of the Middle East, North Africa, and Europe. Each lesson has an introduction to the country being studied that consists of interesting facts about the country, especially focusing on its role in history. Obviously, the current information about the countries is subject to change. There have been recent uprisings and deaths of dictators that could affect this current history, but we have made it as accurate as possible at the time of writing. Students will study world geography in more detail in a later course. The information given about each country now serves merely as an introduction. Students will only be tested on their map work, not on the text facts.

The main goal of this course is for students to master the identification of each country on a map. By the end of the course, students should be able to map each of the countries studied, including all of the capital cities. This requires some review in order for students to retain what they have learned. So when you are studying the countries of Europe, regularly give your students a blank outline map (you can copy the quizzes and tests for multiple use) of the Middle East and North Africa, and have them fill it in.

We usually study 2-3 countries each week. For each country, do the following:

- Using the textbook, students fill in the capital and ancient name for the country.
- Teacher and students read the paragraphs from the text, or students read the material independently.
- Use the full-color flags in the back of the text to color in the line drawings of the flags as you study them.
- In the Fun Facts section of the Student Workbook, choose from any of the following: 1) Record interesting teacher-directed facts about the country using the textbook or other resources for a guide, or 2) Students record their own favorite facts about the country.
- Map Work: Teacher directs the students in marking famous cities or landmarks (i.e., mountains, major rivers, lakes, national parks or monuments, etc.). We use colored pencils for this. Emphasize neatness. Encourage students to take pride in their map. Sometimes the students' maps will have some landmarks already labeled.

Discuss whether the country borders are natural (formed by rivers or mountains) or man-made (straight lines).

Label any countries and oceans or seas that border the country.

There is a quiz after each review lesson in the workbook, and there is a final test to be taken after each unit.

United States Geography:

Students normally take this geography course after they have learned the United States and their capitals (Memoria Press' *States and Capitals*). To aid in retention of this knowledge, we review them throughout this year using the Memoria Press *United States Geography Review Workbook*, a supplement to this course.

MEMORIA PRESS
www.MemoriaPress.com

GEOGRAPHY I
The Middle East, North Africa, & Europe
TEACHER GUIDE
Laura Bateman and Brett Vaden
Contributing Editors: Dayna Grant and Michael Simpson
ISBN 978-1-61538-125-8

CONTENTS

The Middle East, North Africa, & Europe

Middle East ... 6
Israel ... 7
Jordan ... 8
Syria ... 9
Lebanon ... 10
Iraq ... 11
Iran ... 12
Turkey ... 13
Saudi Arabia ... 14
Afghanistan ... 15
Pakistan ... 16
Review ... 17

North Africa ... 22
Egypt ... 23
Sudan ... 24
Libya ... 25
Tunisia ... 26
Algeria ... 27
Morocco ... 28
Review ... 29

Mediterranean Europe ... 32
Greece ... 33
Italy ... 34
Spain ... 35
Portugal ... 36
Review ... 37

Central Europe ... 40
France ... 41
Switzerland & Liechtenstein ... 42
Austria ... 43
Germany ... 44
Review ... 45

The British Isles and the Low Countries ... 48
Netherlands ... 49
Belgium & Luxembourg ... 50
United Kingdom ... 51
Ireland ... 52
Review ... 53

Review Europe Part I ... 55

Scandinavia ... 60
Norway ... 61
Sweden ... 62
Denmark ... 63
Iceland ... 64
Finland ... 65
Review ... 66

Eastern Europe: Part I ... 70
Russia ... 71
Estonia ... 72
Latvia ... 73
Lithuania ... 74
Belarus ... 75
Ukraine ... 76
Poland ... 77
Review ... 78

Eastern Europe: Part II ... 80
The Czech Republic ... 80
Slovakia ... 81
Hungary ... 82
Romania & Moldova ... 83
Bulgaria ... 84
Albania ... 85
The Balkans ... 86
Review ... 87

Review Scandinavia & Eastern Europe ... 89
Review Europe ... 92

Appendix ... 95
Countries & Capitals ... 97
Reproducible Maps ... 99

Quizzes and Tests ... 103
Quizzes and Tests Key ... 123

MIDDLE EAST

MIDDLE EAST

Look at the map below. Identify each country.

1. Turkey
2. Saudi Arabia
3. Iran
4. Afghanistan
5. Jordan
6. Syria
7. Lebanon
8. Iraq
9. Israel
10. Pakistan

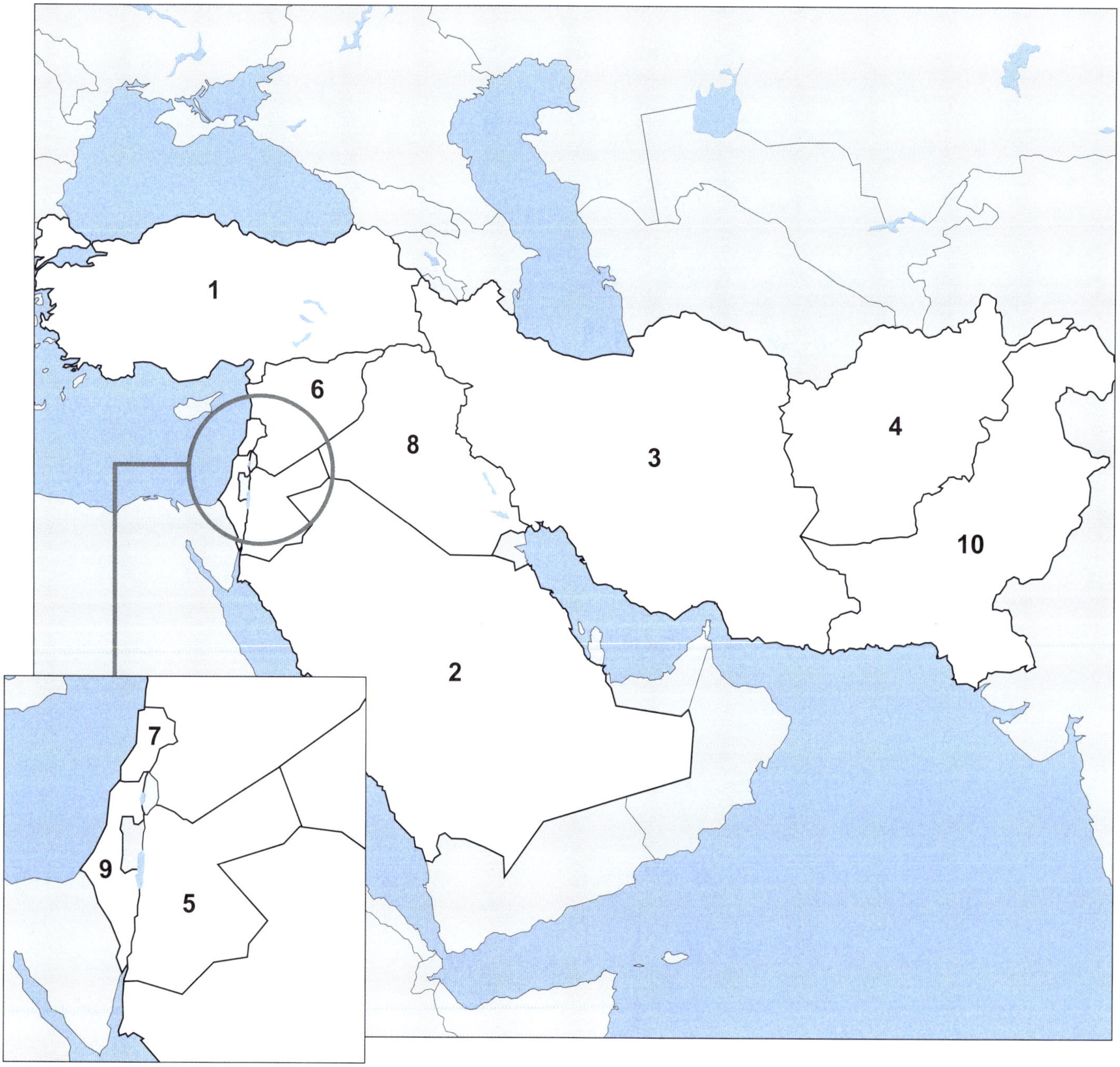

ISRAEL

Country: Israel Capital: Jerusalem Ancient Name: Israel (The Holy Land)

Fun Facts: Answers will vary.

Copy the name of the country and its capital three times. Pay close attention to correct spelling.

1. ______________________________

2. ______________________________

3. ______________________________

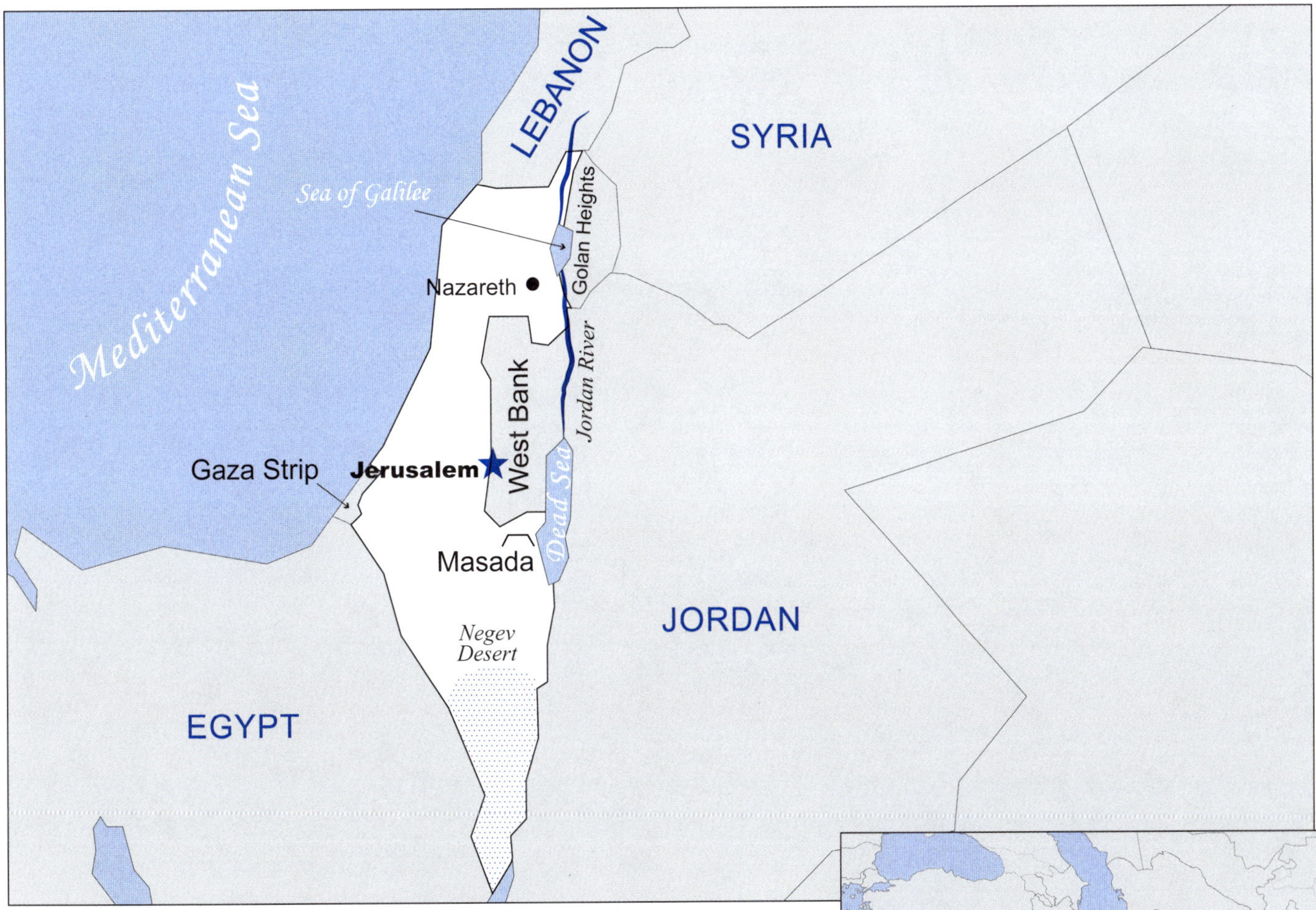

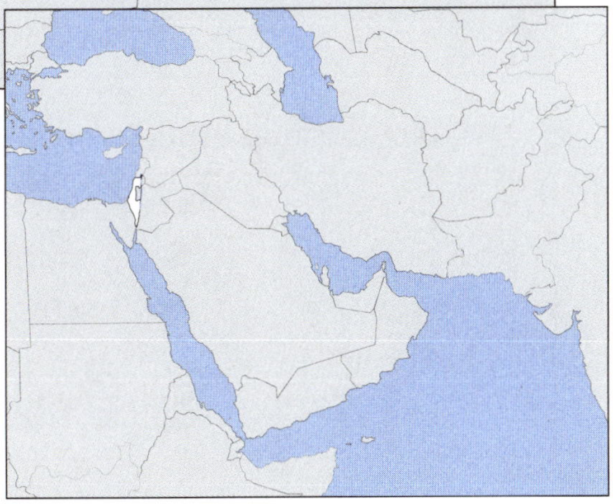

Label the map using terms from the word bank.

WORD BANK

Jerusalem	Jordan River	Negev Desert
Egypt	Dead Sea	West Bank
Lebanon	Jordan	Mediterranean Sea
Nazareth	Syria	Gaza Strip
Sea of Galilee	Masada	Golan Heights

JORDAN

Country: Jordan Capital: Amman Ancient Name: Edom, Moab, Nabataea

Fun Facts: Answers will vary.

Copy the name of the country and its capital three times. Pay close attention to correct spelling.

1. ____________________
2. ____________________
3. ____________________

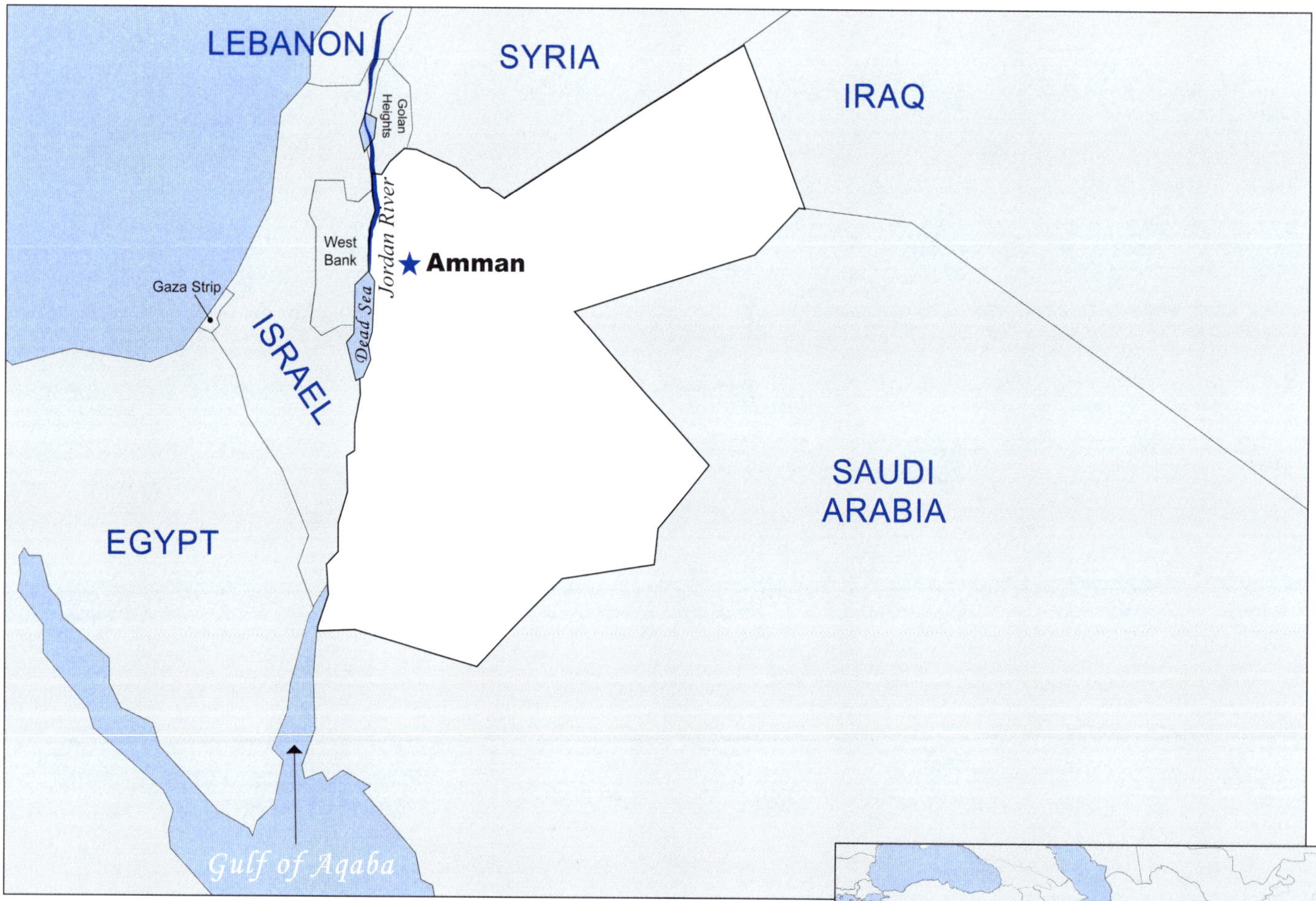

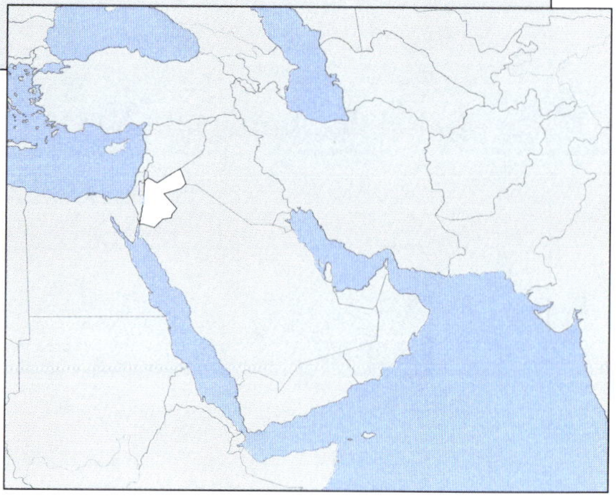

Label the map using terms from the word bank.

WORD BANK		
Amman	Saudi Arabia	Jordan River
Syria	Israel	Dead Sea
Lebanon	Egypt	
Iraq	Gulf of Aqaba	

SYRIA

Country: Syria Capital: Damascus Ancient Name: Aram

Fun Facts: Answers will vary.

Copy the name of the country and its capital three times. Pay close attention to correct spelling.

1. ______

2. ______

3. ______

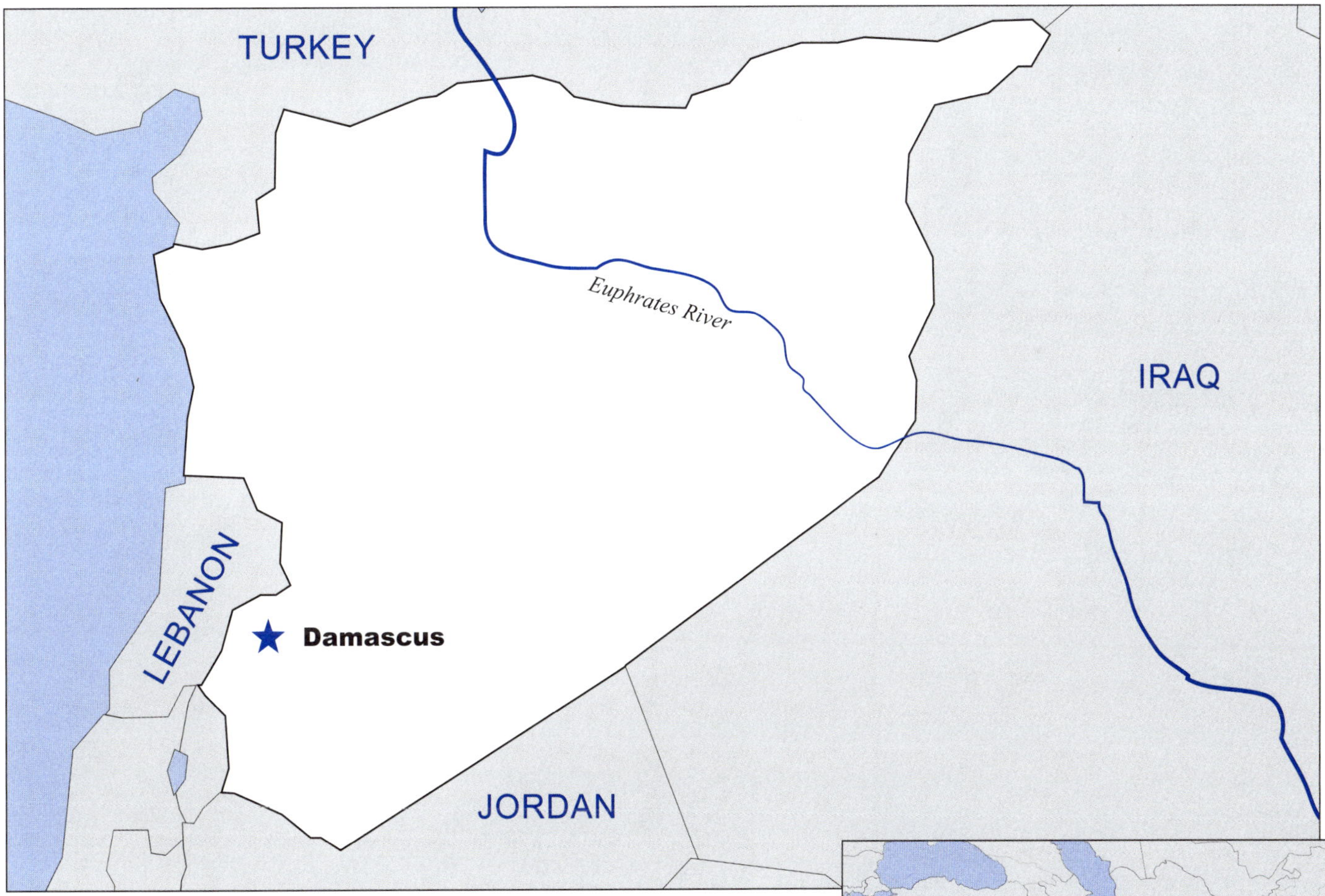

Label the map using terms from the word bank.

WORD BANK		
Damascus	Jordan	Euphrates River
Lebanon	Turkey	Iraq

LEBANON

Country: Lebanon Capital: Beirut Ancient Name: Phoenicia

Fun Facts: Answers will vary.

Copy the name of the country and its capital three times. Pay close attention to correct spelling.

1. ______

2. ______

3. ______

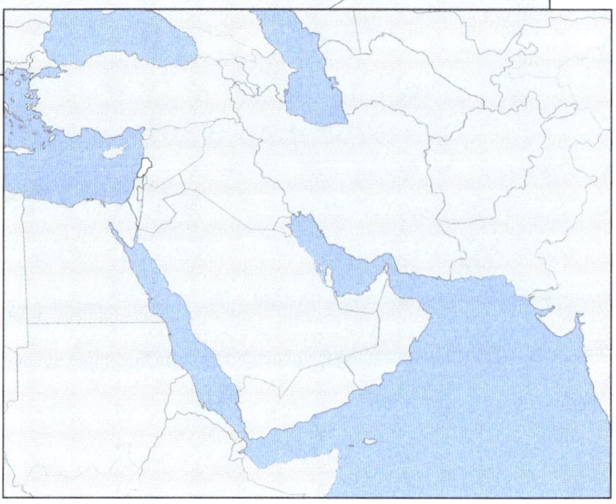

Label the map using terms from the word bank.

WORD BANK	
Syria	Israel
Mediterranean Sea	Golan Heights
Beirut	Tyrc
Sidon	

IRAQ

Country: Iraq Capital: Baghdad Ancient Name: Assyria and Babylon

Fun Facts: Answers will vary.

Copy the name of the country and its capital three times. Pay close attention to correct spelling.

1. ______________________________

2. ______________________________

3. ______________________________

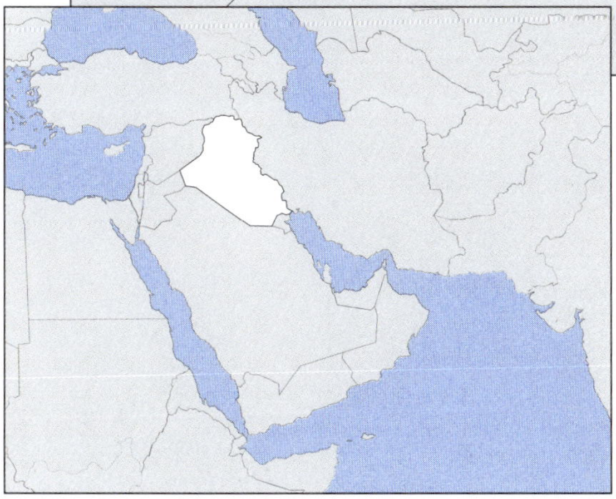

Label the map using terms from the word bank.

WORD BANK

Syria	Baghdad	Kuwait
Turkey	Tigris River	Persian Gulf
Iran	Euphrates River	Shatt al-Arab

IRAN

Country: Iran Capital: Tehran Ancient Name: Persia

Fun Facts: Answers will vary.

Copy the name of the country and its capital three times. Pay close attention to correct spelling.

1. ______________________________

2. ______________________________

3. ______________________________

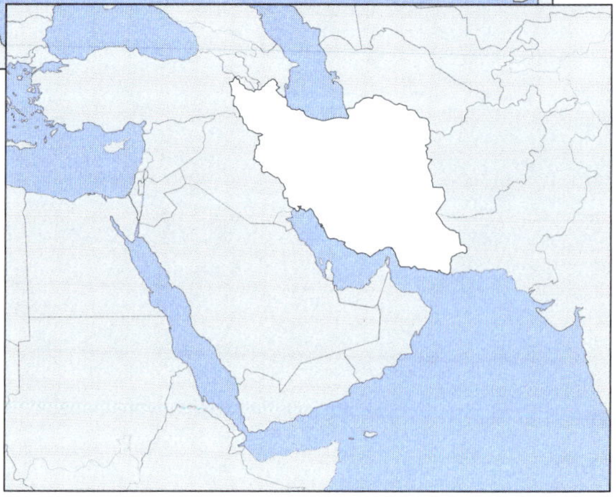

Label the map using terms from the word bank.

WORD BANK		
Caspian Sea	Saudi Arabia	Afghanistan
Iraq	Kuwait	Pakistan
Tehran	Persian Gulf	

TURKEY

Country: Turkey Capital: Ankara Ancient Name: Asia Minor

Fun Facts: Answers will vary.

Copy the name of the country and its capital three times. Pay close attention to correct spelling.

1. ____________________

2. ____________________

3. ____________________

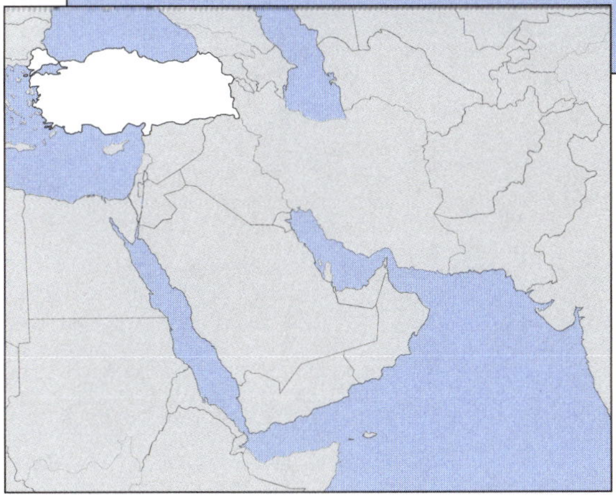

Label the map using terms from the word bank.

WORD BANK		
Istanbul	Euphrates River	Black Sea
Mediterranean Sea	Tigris River	Dardanelles
Aegean Sea	Iraq	
Syria	Ankara	

SAUDI ARABIA

Country: Saudi Arabia Capital: Riyadh Ancient Name: Arabia

Fun Facts: Answers will vary.

Copy the name of the country and its capital three times. Pay close attention to correct spelling.

1. ______________________________

2. ______________________________

3. ______________________________

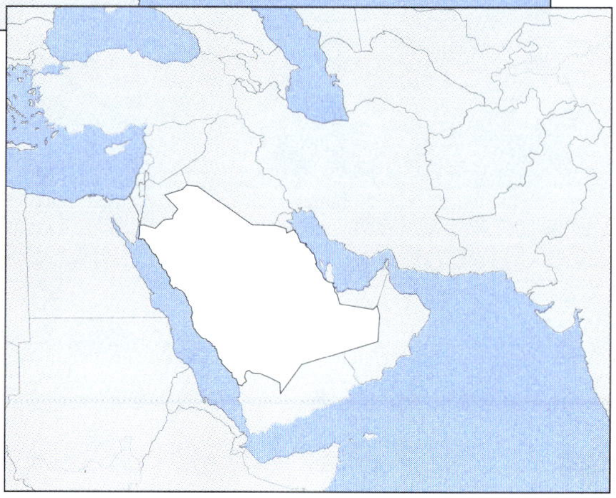

Label the map using terms from the word bank.

WORD BANK

Medina	Riyadh	Kuwait
Mecca	Persian Gulf	Yemen
Red Sea	Iran	Egypt
Arabian Sea	Iraq	Sudan
Oman	Jordan	U.A.E.

PAKISTAN

Country: Pakistan Capital: Islamabad Ancient Name: Indus

Fun Facts: Answers will vary.

Copy the name of the country and its capital three times. Pay close attention to correct spelling.

1. ____________________
2. ____________________
3. ____________________

Label the map using terms from the word bank.

WORD BANK		
Islamabad	Iran	Indus River
India	China	Karachi
Arabian Sea	Afghanistan	

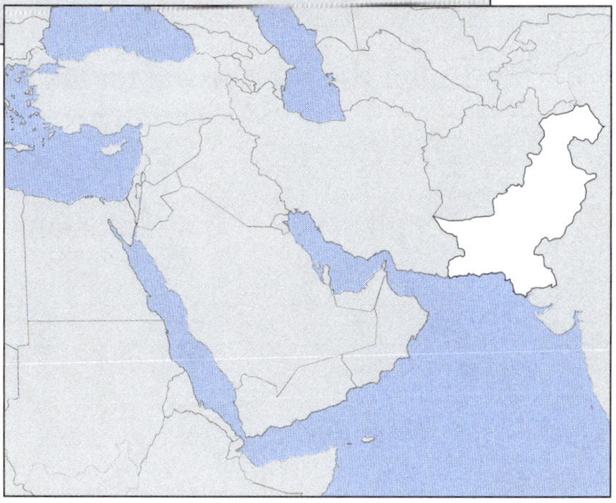

AFGHANISTAN

Country: Afghanistan Capital: Kabul Ancient Name: N/A

Fun Facts: Answers will vary.

Copy the name of the country and its capital three times. Pay close attention to correct spelling.

1. ______

2. ______

3. ______

Label the map using terms from the word bank.

WORD BANK		
Kabul	Pakistan	Iran

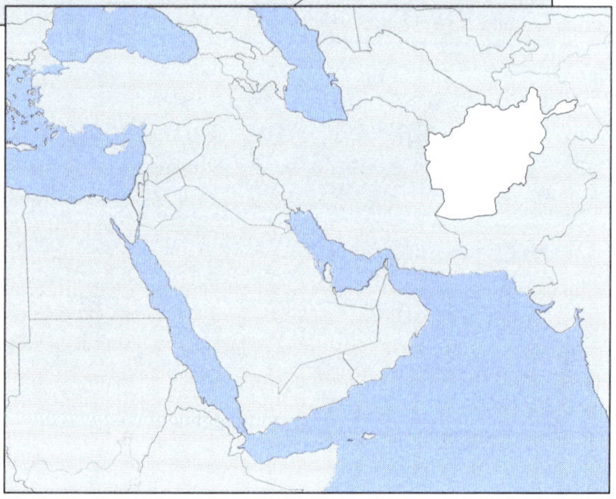

REVIEW

Middle East

On the map below, label and color each of the countries you have studied.

***Note to Teachers*:**
Students should color each of the labeled countries a different color. The rest of the countries should be colored the same color. If time allows, the bodies of water surrounding the continents could be labeled.

REVIEW

Middle East

Copy the names of the countries and their capitals below. Pay close attention to correct spelling.

1. Country: Turkey — Capital: Ankara
2. Country: Iran — Capital: Tehran
3. Country: Afghanistan — Capital: Kabul
4. Country: Pakistan — Capital: Islamabad
5. Country: Saudi Arabia — Capital: Riyadh
6. Country: Jordan — Capital: Amman
7. Country: Israel — Capital: Jerusalem
8. Country: Lebanon — Capital: Beirut
9. Country: Syria — Capital: Damascus
10. Country: Iraq — Capital: Baghdad

Use the map on the next page to practice identifying the countries.

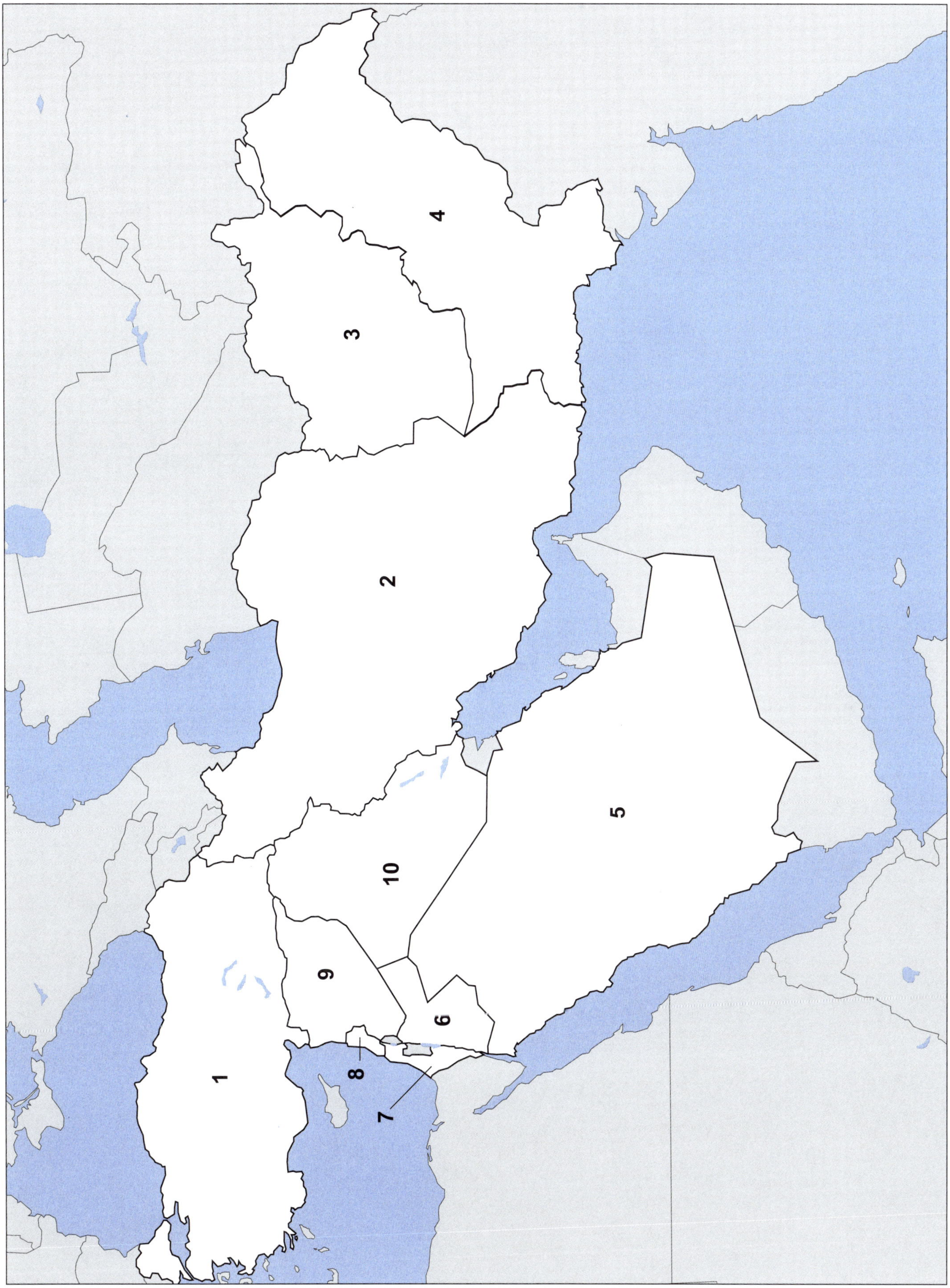
4
3
2
5
10
1
9
6
8
7

NORTH AFRICA

NORTH AFRICA

Look at the map below. Identify each country.

1. Libya
2. Algeria
3. Tunisia
4. Sudan
5. Morocco
6. Egypt
7. South Sudan

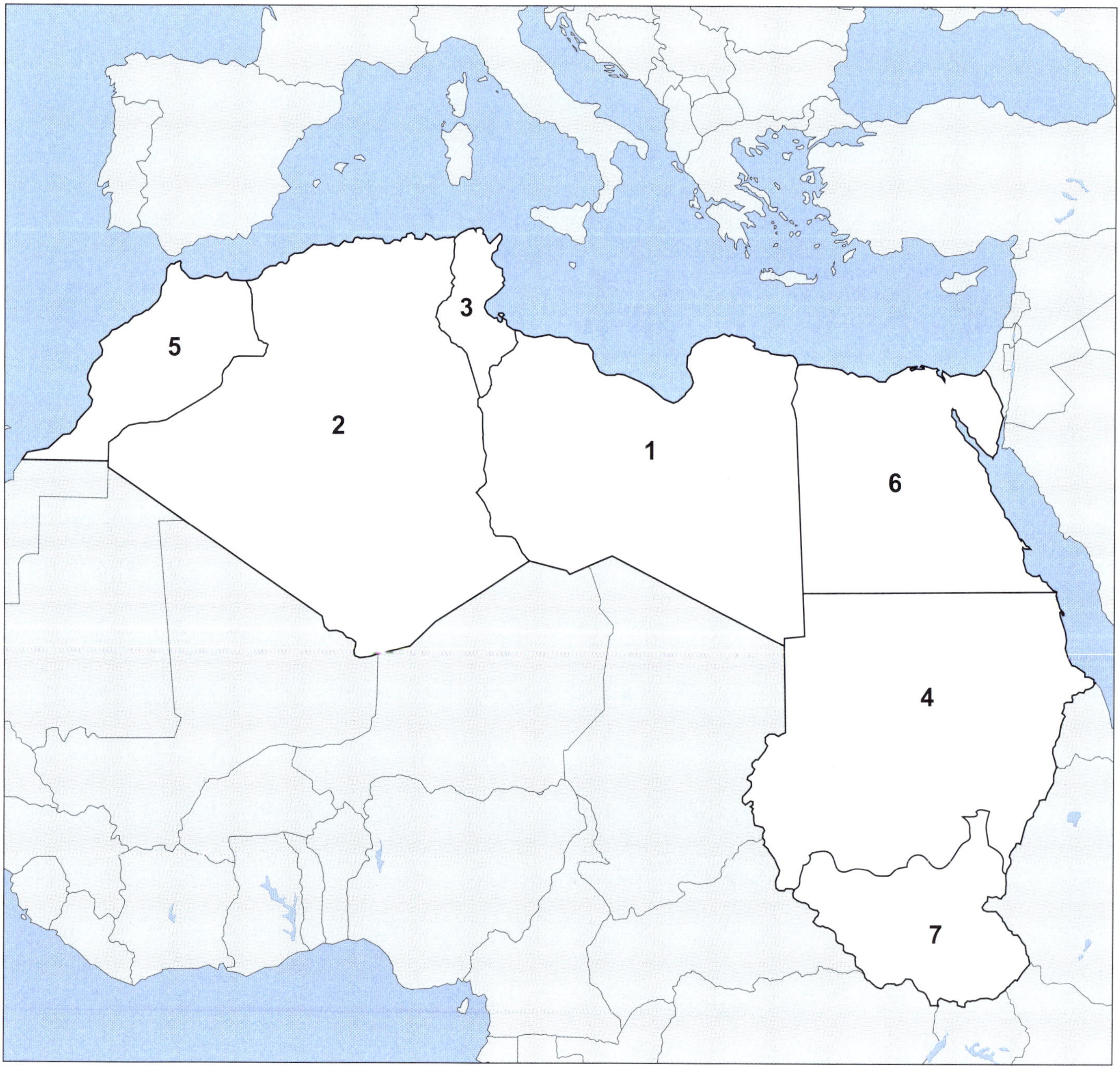

EGYPT

Country: Egypt Capital: Cairo Ancient Name: Gift of the Nile

Fun Facts: Answers will vary.

Copy the name of the country and its capital three times. Pay close attention to correct spelling.

1. ____________________
2. ____________________
3. ____________________

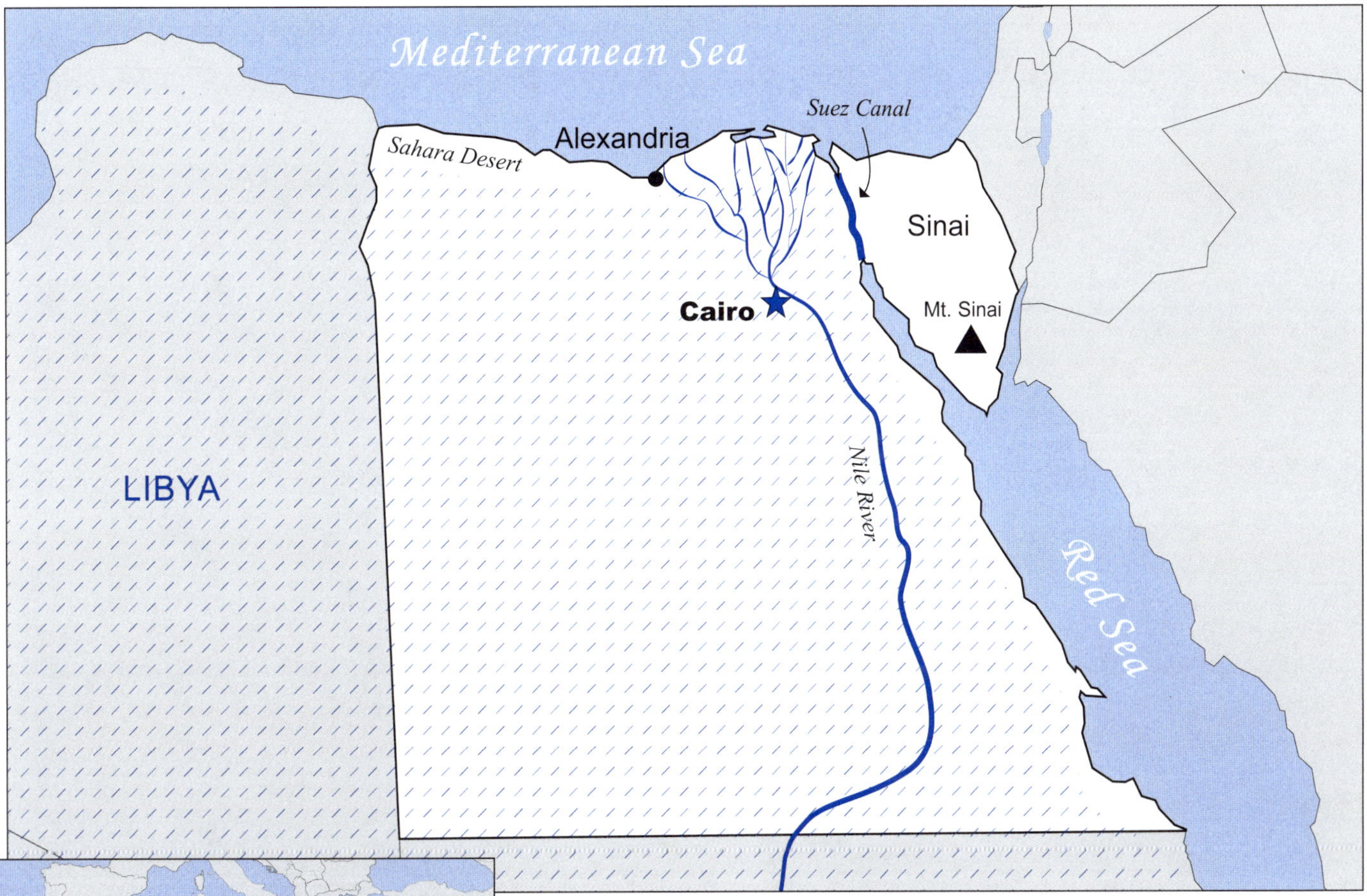

Label the map using terms from the word bank.

WORD BANK		
Nile River	Cairo	Mediterranean Sea
Sinai	Red Sea	Sahara Desert
Alexandria	Mt. Sinai	
Libya	Suez Canal	

SUDAN & SOUTH SUDAN

Country: Sudan Capital: Khartoum Ancient Name: Kush

Country: South Sudan Capital: Juba Ancient Name: Kush

Fun Facts: Answers will vary.

Copy the name of the countries and their capitals three times. Pay close attention to correct spelling.

1. ____________ 1. ____________

2. ____________ 2. ____________

3. ____________ 3. ____________

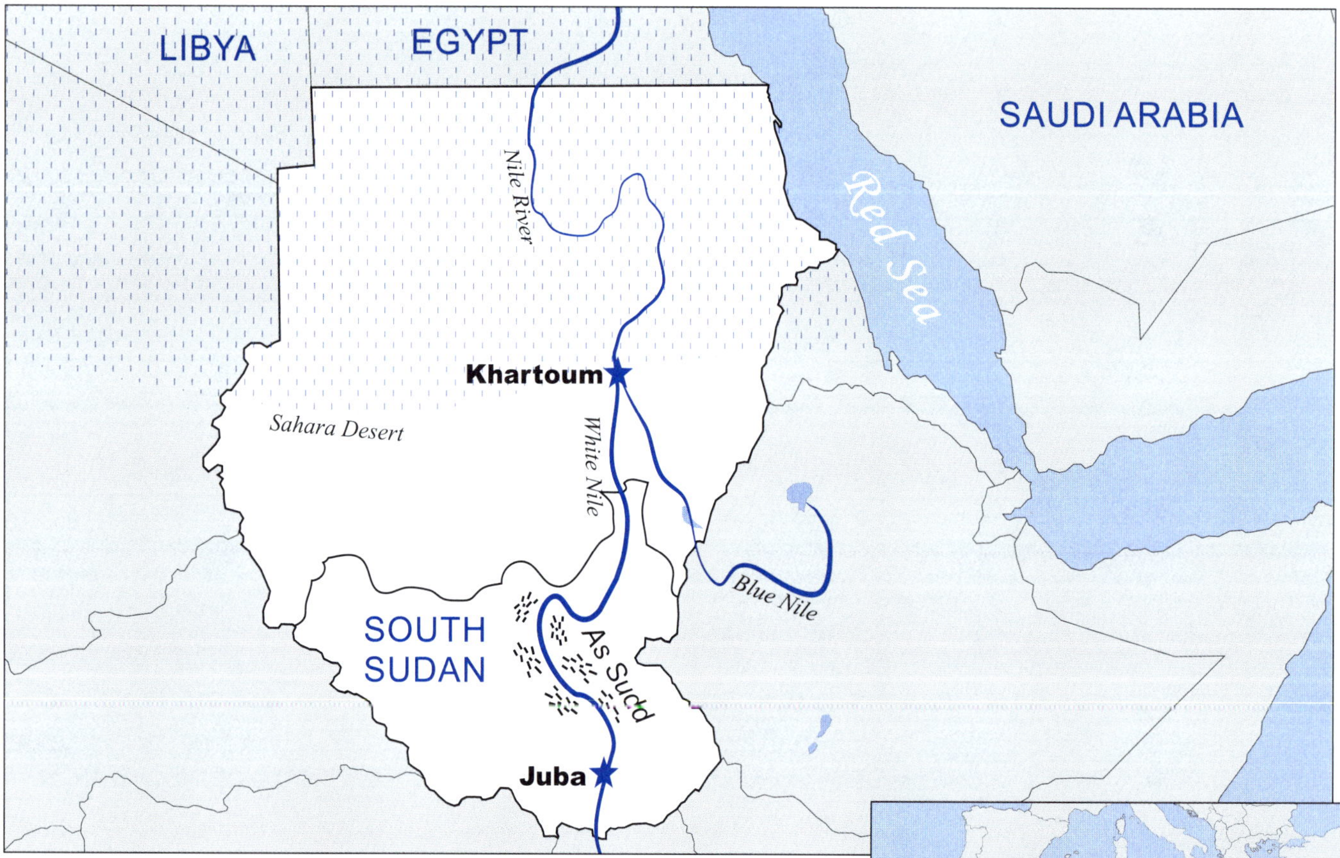

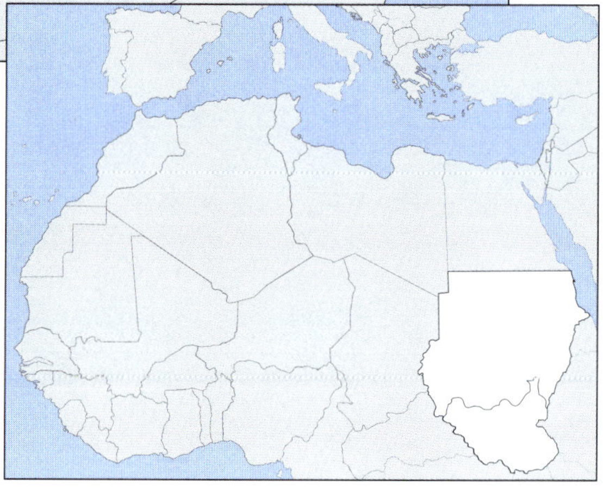

Label the map using terms from the word bank.

WORD BANK		
Blue Nile	Saudi Arabia	Juba
South Sudan	Egypt	White Nile
Red Sea	Nile River	As Sudd
Khartoum	Libya	Sahara Desert

LIBYA

Country: Libya Capital: Tripoli Ancient Name: The Shores of Tripoli

Fun Facts: Answers will vary.

Copy the name of the country and its capital three times. Pay close attention to correct spelling.

1. ______________________
2. ______________________
3. ______________________

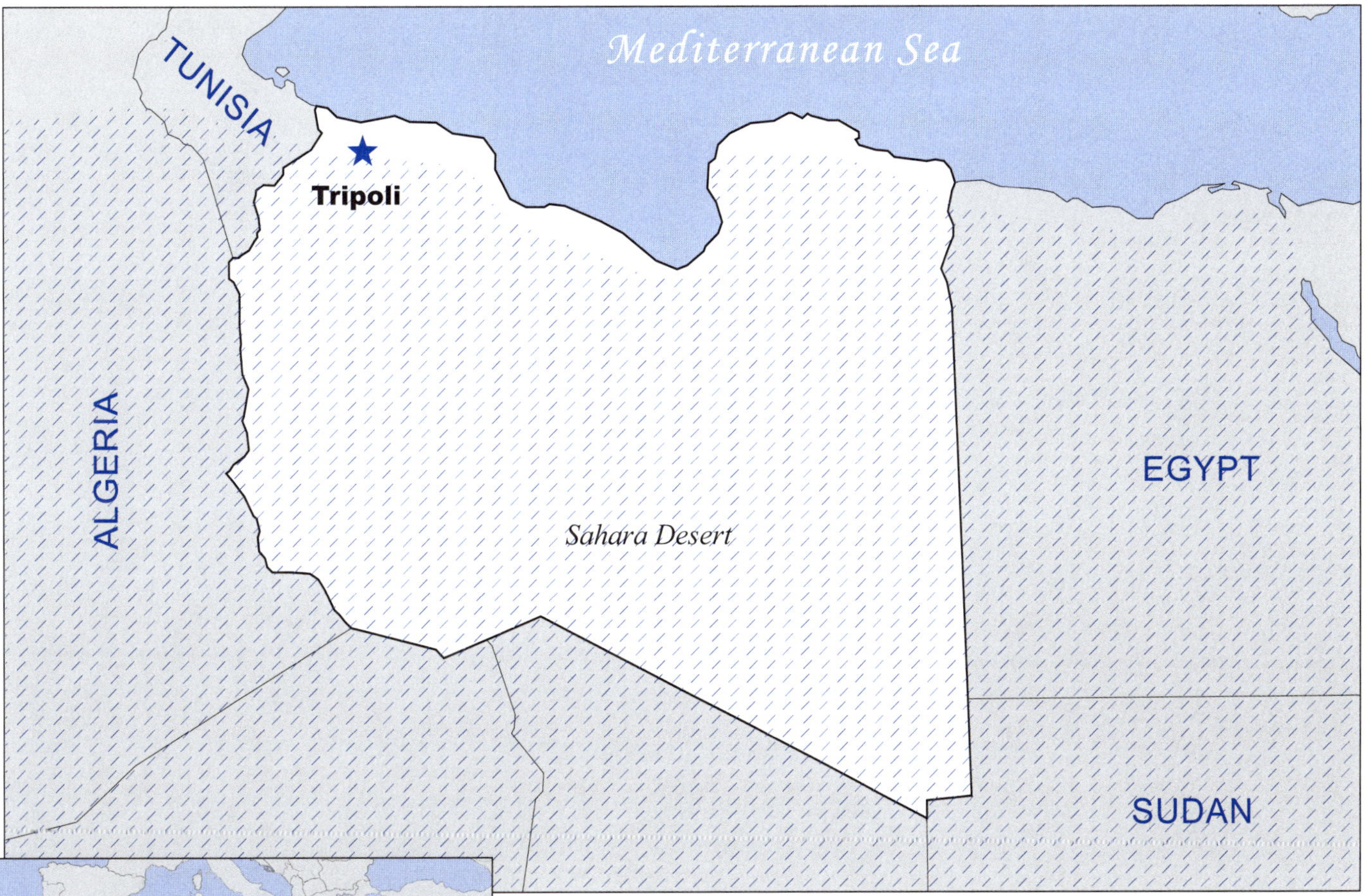

Label the map using terms from the word bank.

WORD BANK		
Egypt	Mediterranean Sea	Tunisia
Sudan	Algeria	Sahara Desert
	Tripoli	

TUNISIA

Country: Tunisia Capital: Tunis Ancient Name: Carthage

Fun Facts: Answers will vary.

Copy the name of the country and its capital three times. Pay close attention to correct spelling.

1. ______________________________
2. ______________________________
3. ______________________________

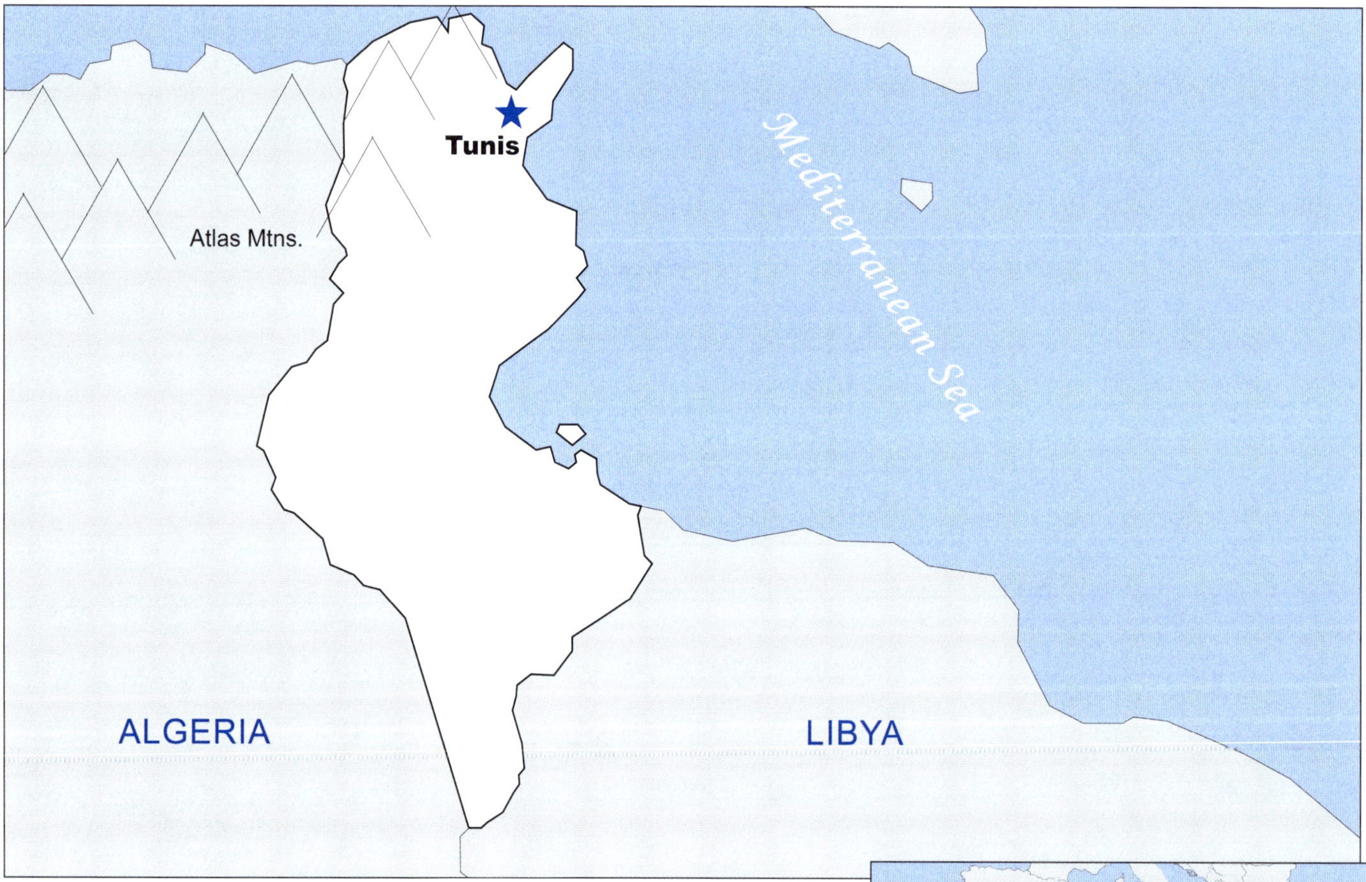

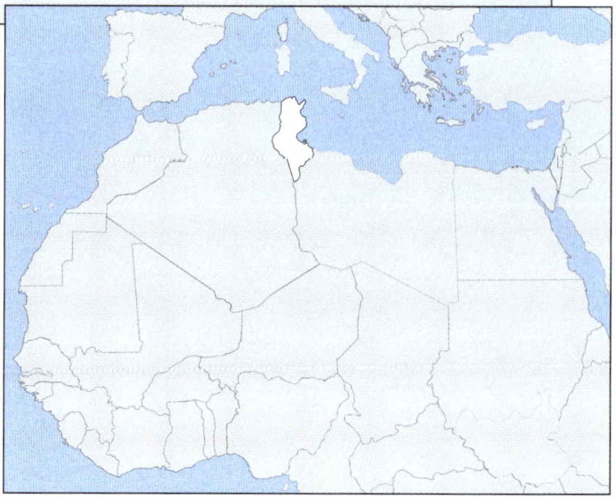

Label the map using terms from the word bank.

WORD BANK	
Algeria	Tunis
Libya	Mediterranean Sea

ALGERIA

Country: Algeria Capital: Algiers Ancient Name: Numidia

Fun Facts: Answers will vary.

Copy the name of the country and its capital three times. Pay close attention to correct spelling.

1. ______________________

2. ______________________

3. ______________________

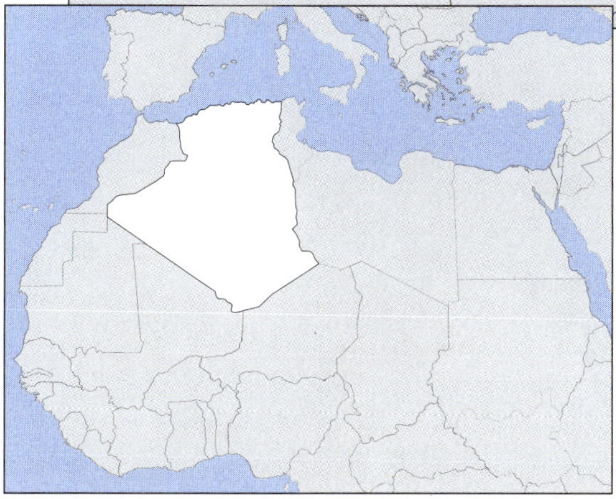

Label the map using terms from the word bank.

WORD BANK		
Sahara Desert	Tunisia	Mediterranean Sea
Morocco	Libya	
Algiers	Atlantic Ocean	

MOROCCO

Country: Morocco Capital: Rabat Ancient Name: Mauretania or "The Farthest West"

Fun Facts: Answers will vary.

Copy the name of the country and its capital three times. Pay close attention to correct spelling.

1. ______________________________

2. ______________________________

3. ______________________________

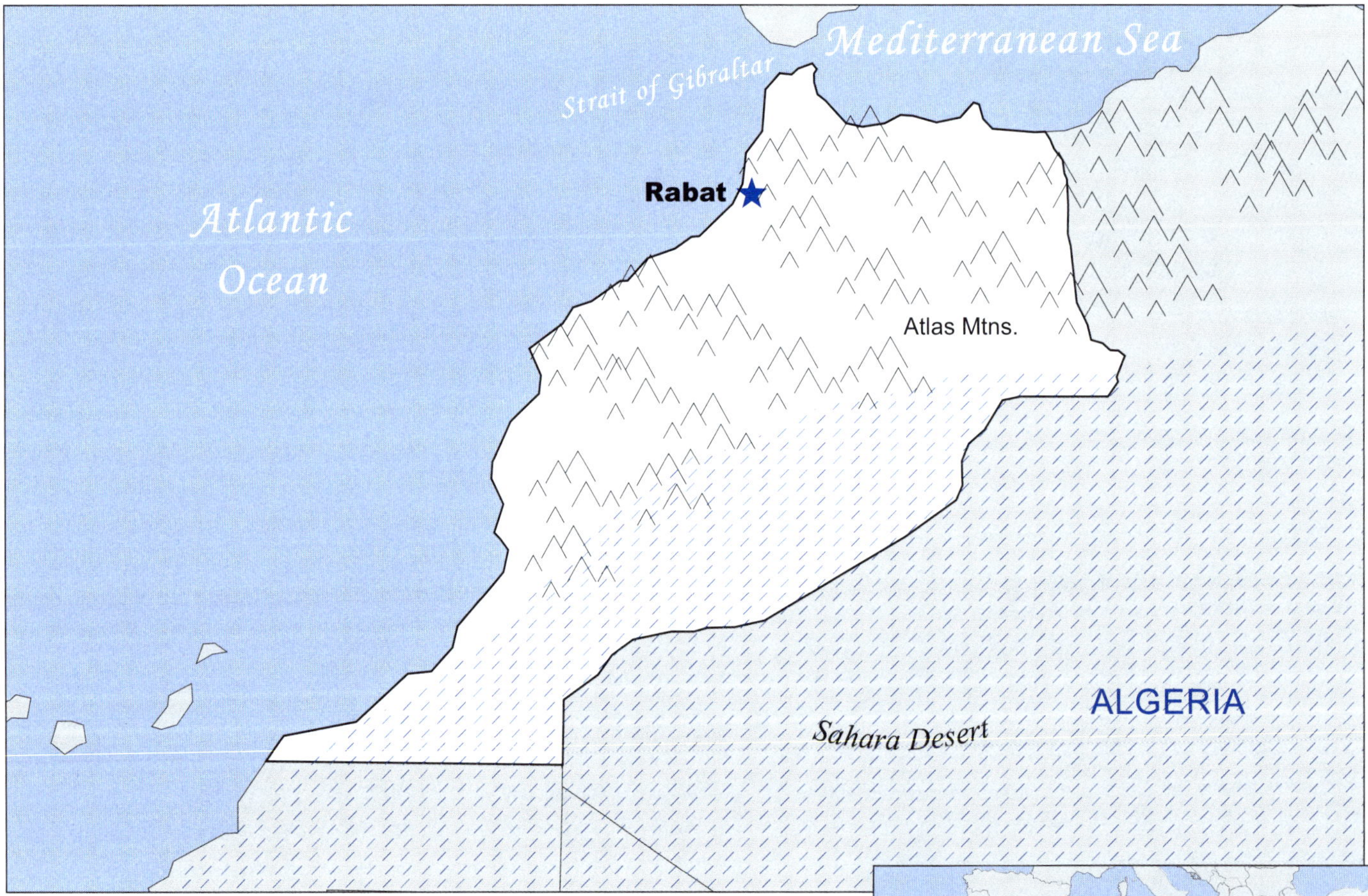

WORD BANK

Algeria
Atlantic Ocean
Mediterranean Sea
Rabat
Strait of Gibraltar

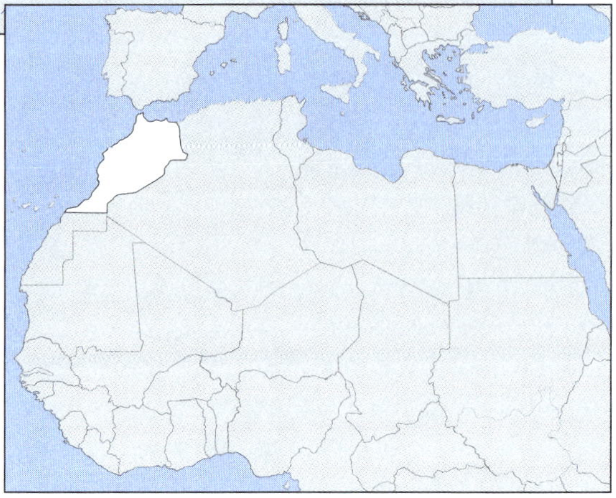

REVIEW

North Africa

On the map below, label and color each of the countries you have studied.

***Note to Teachers*:**

Students should color each of the labeled countries a different color. If time allows, the rest of the countries in Africa should be colored the same color, and the bodies of water labeled.

REVIEW

North Africa

Copy the names of the countries and their capitals below. Pay close attention to correct spelling.

1. Country: Morocco Capital: Rabat
2. Country: Algeria Capital: Algiers
3. Country: Tunisia Capital: Tunis
4. Country: Libya Capital: Tripoli
5. Country: Egypt Capital: Cairo
6. Country: Sudan Capital: Khartoum
7. Country: South Sudan Capital: Juba

Use the map below to practice identifying the countries.

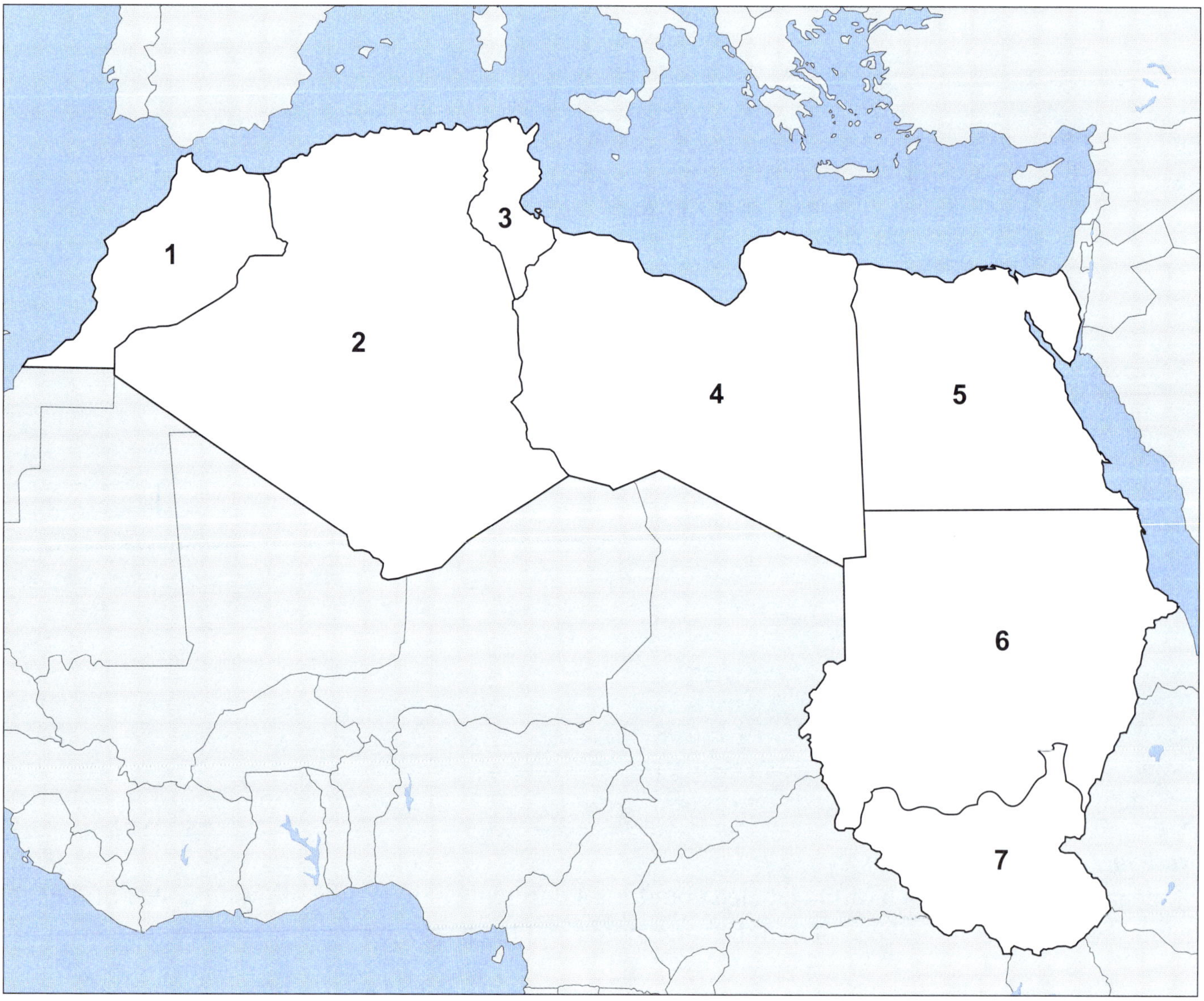

MEDITERRANEAN EUROPE

MEDITERRANEAN EUROPE

Look at the map below. Identify each country.

1. Portugal
2. Italy
3. Spain
4. Greece

GREECE

Country: Greece Capital: Athens Ancient Name: Greece

Fun Facts: Answers will vary.

Copy the name of the country and its capital three times. Pay close attention to correct spelling.

1. ______________________________

2. ______________________________

3. ______________________________

Label the map using terms from the word bank.

WORD BANK

Thessaloniki	Rhodes	Turkey
Athens	Aegean Sea	Albania
Ionian Sea	Mt. Olympus	
Crete	Bulgaria	

ITALY

Country: Italy Capital: Rome Ancient Name: Rome

Fun Facts: Answers will vary.

Copy the name of the country and its capital three times. Pay close attention to correct spelling.

1. ______________________

2. ______________________

3. ______________________

Label the map using terms from the word bank.

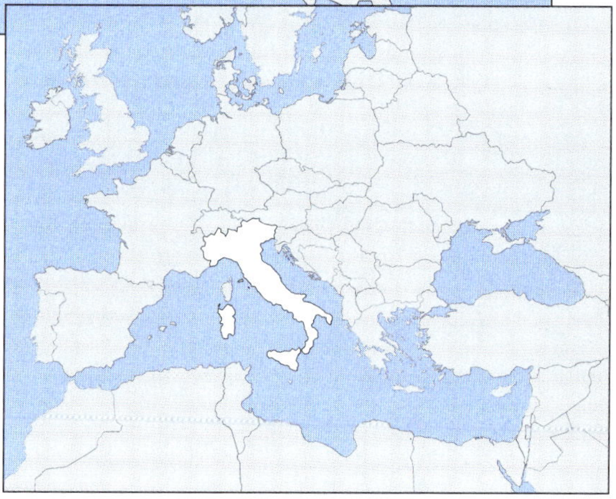

WORD BANK

Switzerland	Sicily	Austria
Rome	France	Po River
Vatican City	Sardinia	Mt. Vesuvius
Venice	Corsica	
Greece	Adriatic Sea	

SPAIN

Country: Spain Capital: Madrid Ancient Name: Hispania

Fun Facts: Answers will vary.

Copy the name of the country and its capital three times. Pay close attention to correct spelling.

1. ____
2. ____
3. ____

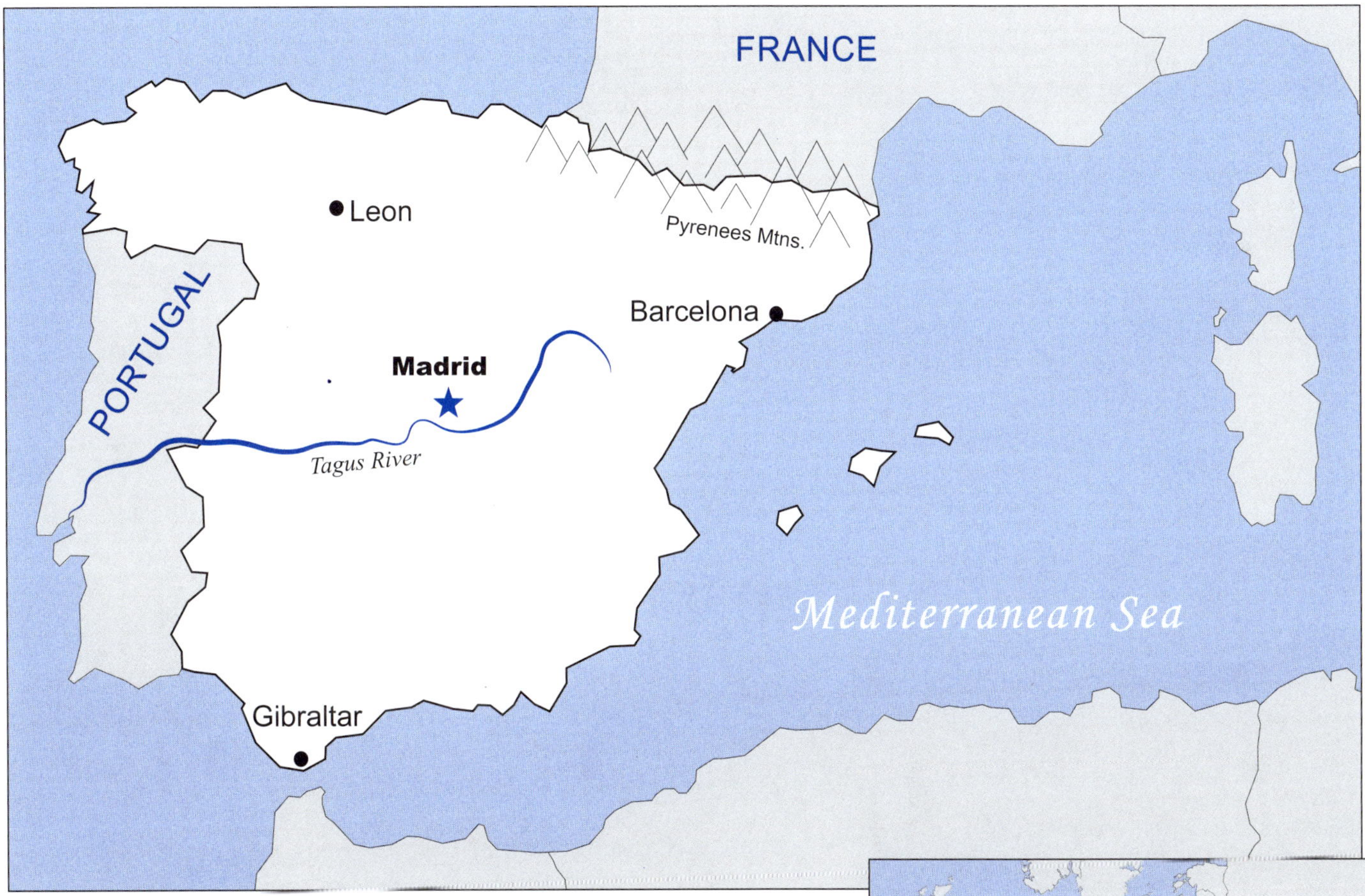

Label the map using terms from the word bank.

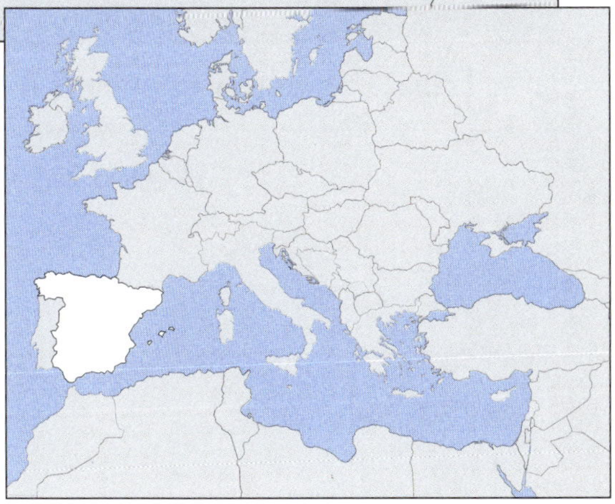

WORD BANK

Leon	Gibraltar	Mediterranean Sea
Tagus River	Barcelona	Madrid
Portugal	France	

PORTUGAL

Country: Portugal Capital: Lisbon Ancient Name: Lusitania

Fun Facts: Answers will vary.

Copy the name of the country and its capital three times. Pay close attention to correct spelling.

1. ____________________

2. ____________________

3. ____________________

Label the map using terms from the word bank.

WORD BANK	
Atlantic Ocean	Spain
Lisbon	Tagus River

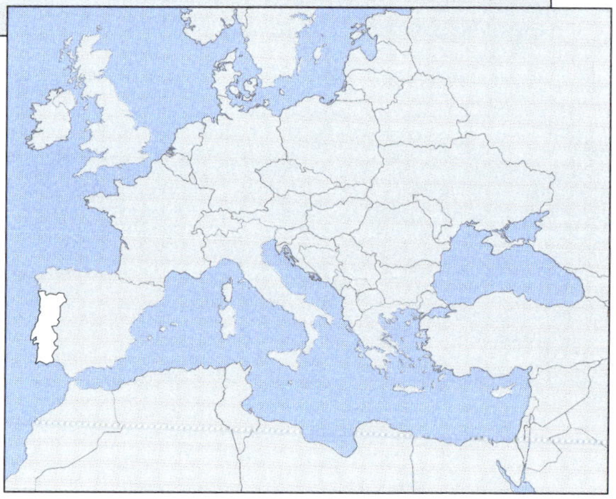

REVIEW

Mediterranean Europe

On the map below, label and color each of the countries you have studied.

***Note to Teachers*:**
Students should color each of the labeled countries a different color. If time allows, the rest of the countries should be colored the same color, and the bodies of water labeled.

REVIEW

Mediterranean Europe

Copy the names of the countries and their capitals below. Pay close attention to correct spelling.

1. Country: Greece Capital: Athens
2. Country: Italy Capital: Rome
3. Country: Spain Capital: Madrid
4. Country: Portugal Capital: Lisbon

Use the map below to practice identifying the countries.

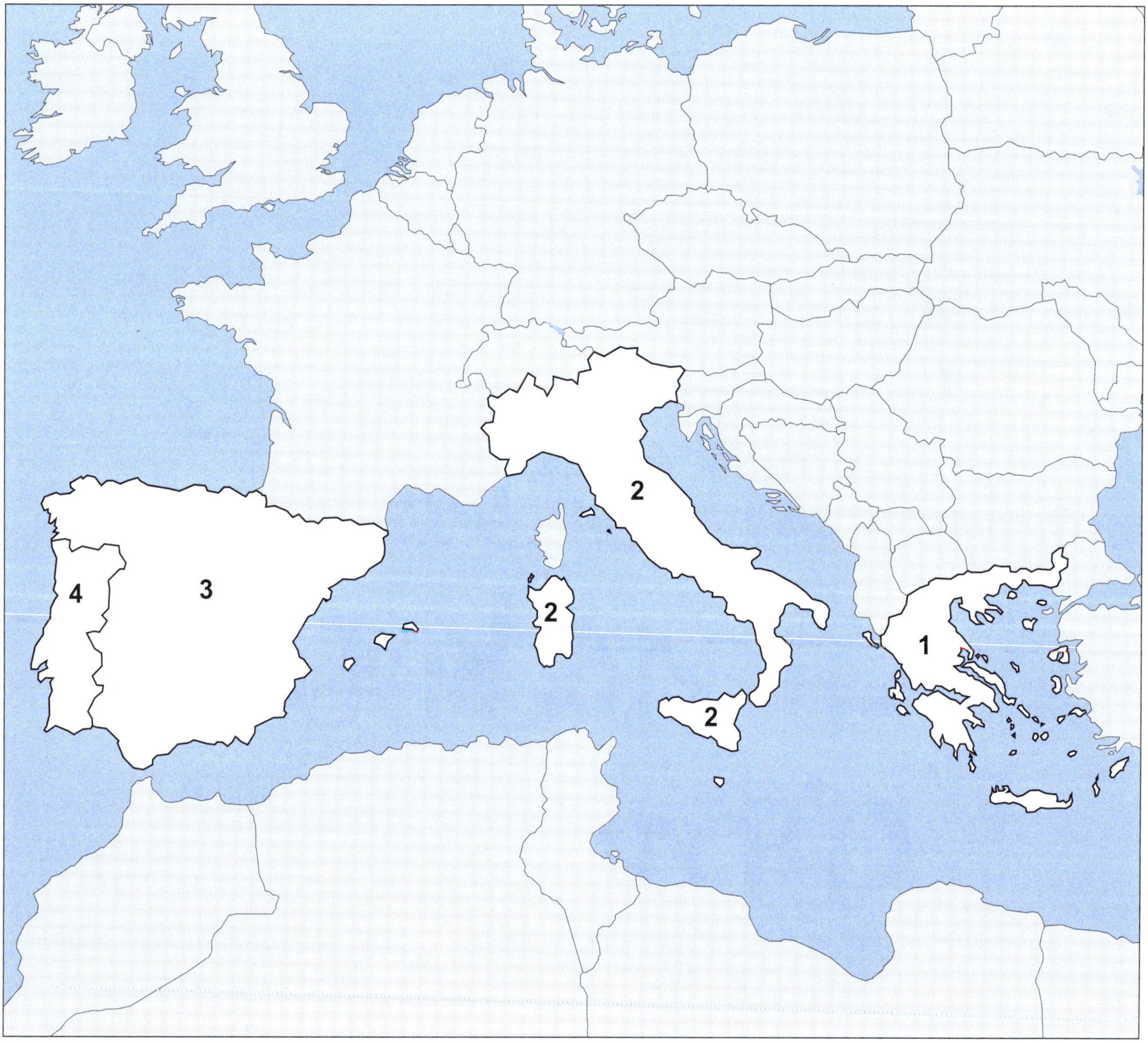

CENTRAL EUROPE

CENTRAL EUROPE

Look at the map below. Identify each country.

1. France
2. Germany
3. Switzerland
4. Austria
5. Liechtenstein

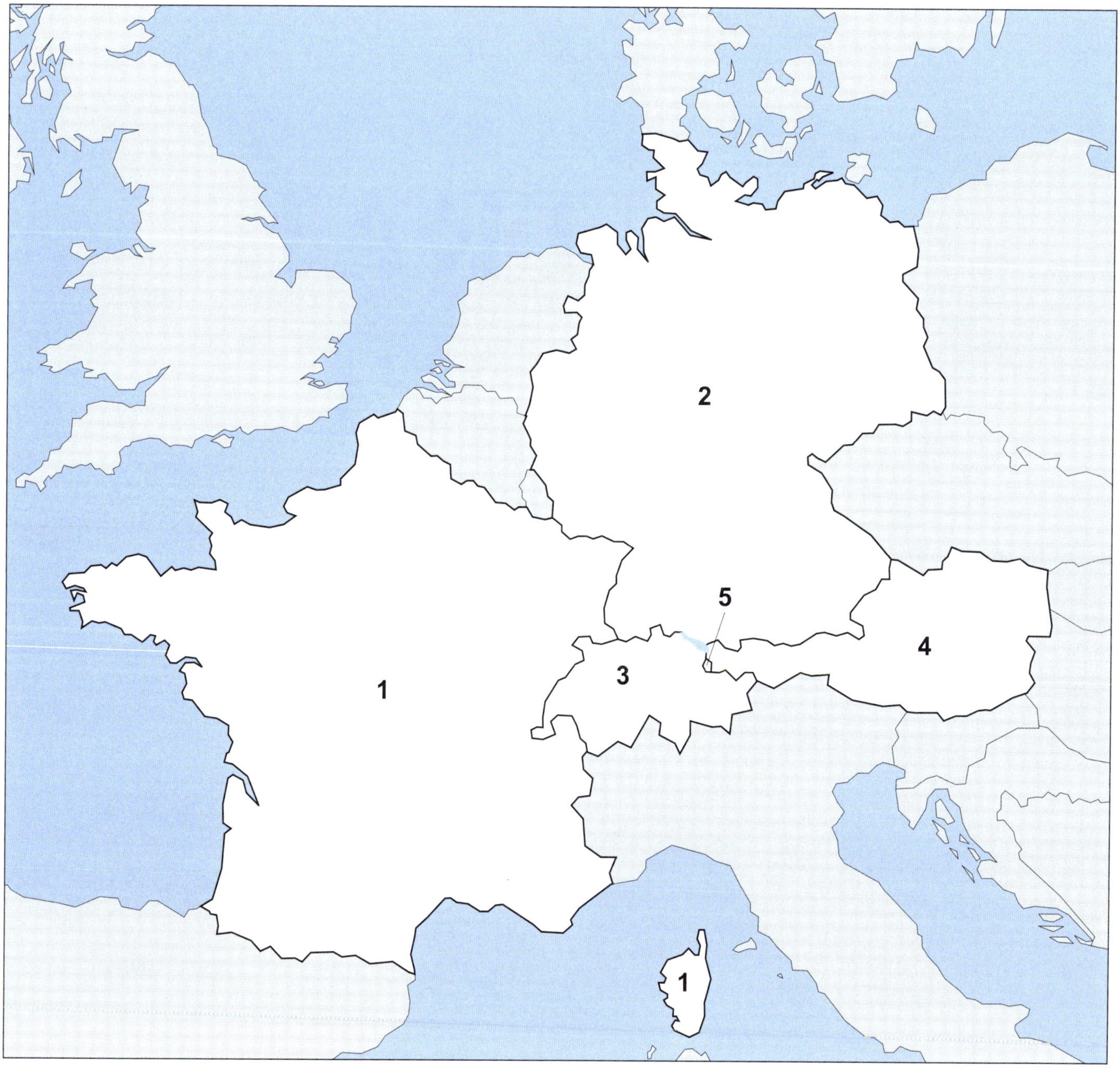

FRANCE

Country: France Capital: Paris Ancient Name: Gaul

Fun Facts: Answers will vary.

Copy the name of the country and its capital three times. Pay close attention to correct spelling.

1. ______

2. ______

3. ______

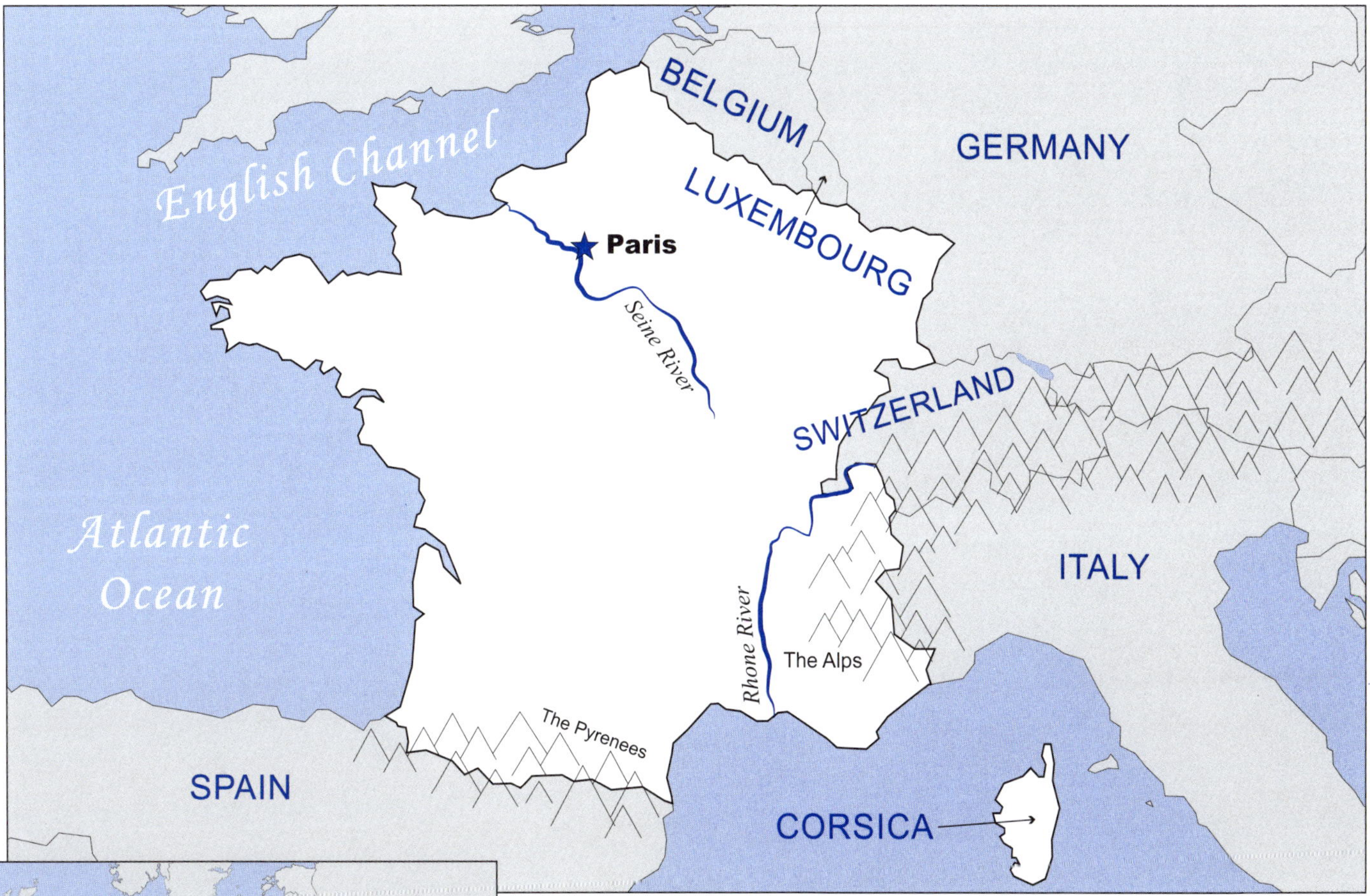

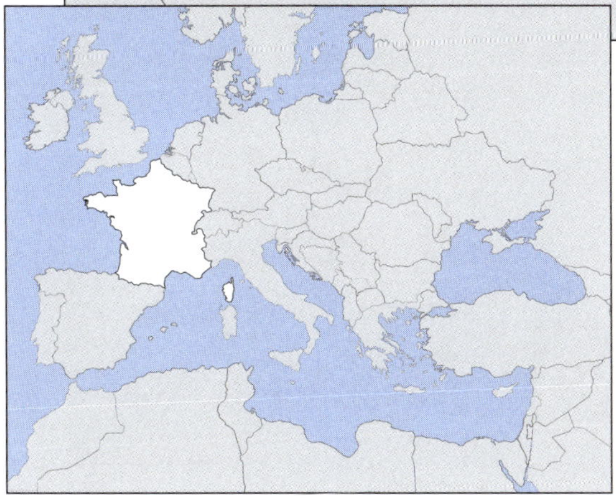

Label the map using terms from the word bank.

WORD BANK

Rhone River	English Channel	Belgium
Italy	Spain	Corsica
Switzerland	The Alps	Atlantic Ocean
Luxembourg	Paris	
Germany	Seine River	

SWITZERLAND & LIECHTENSTEIN

Country: Switzerland Capital: Bern Ancient Name: Land of the Helvetii

Country: Liechtenstein Capital: Vaduz Ancient Name: Land of the Helvetii

Fun Facts: Answers will vary.

Copy the name of the countries and their capitals three times. Pay close attention to correct spelling.

1. ______________________ 1. ______________________

2. ______________________ 2. ______________________

3. ______________________ 3. ______________________

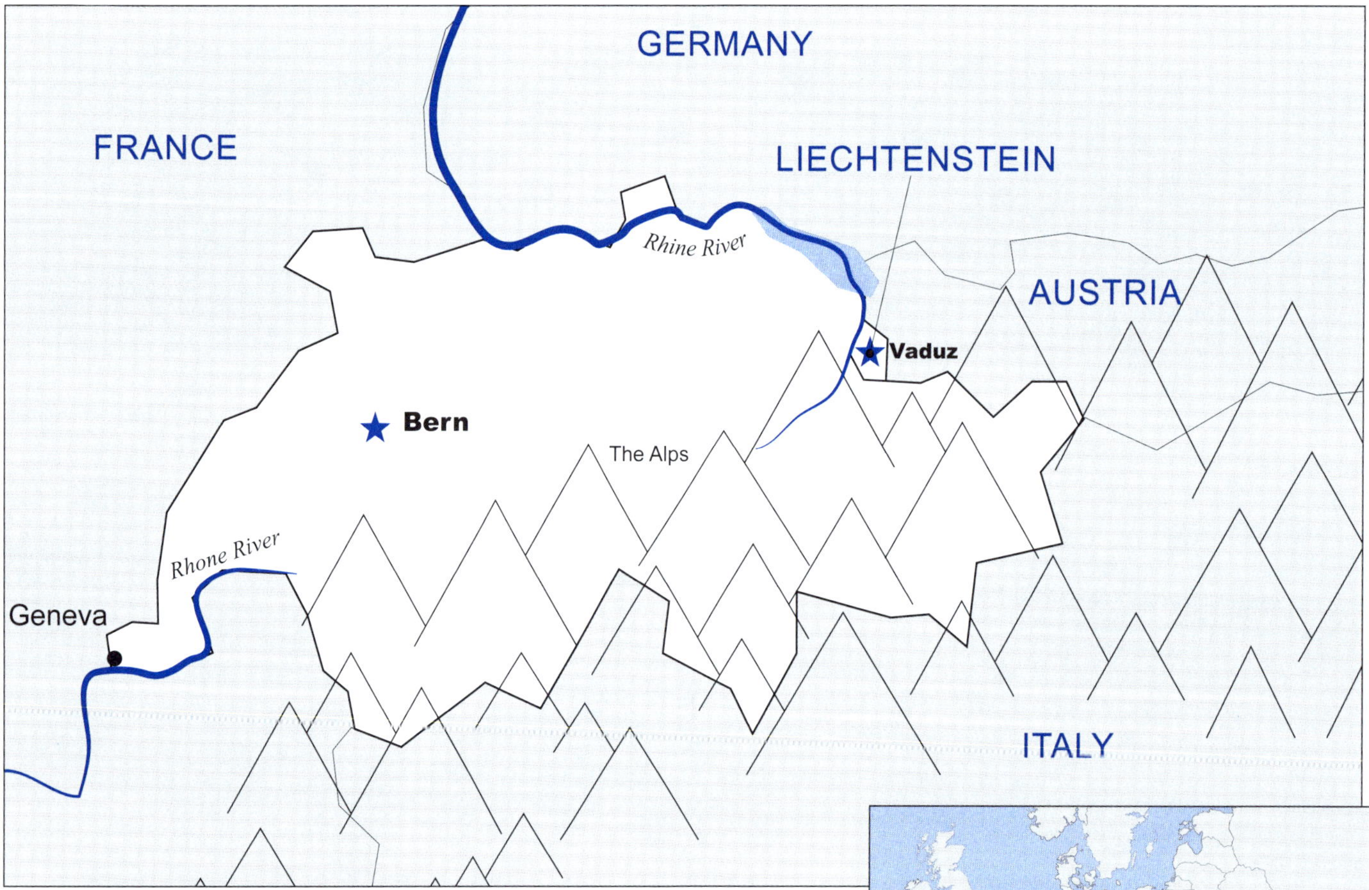

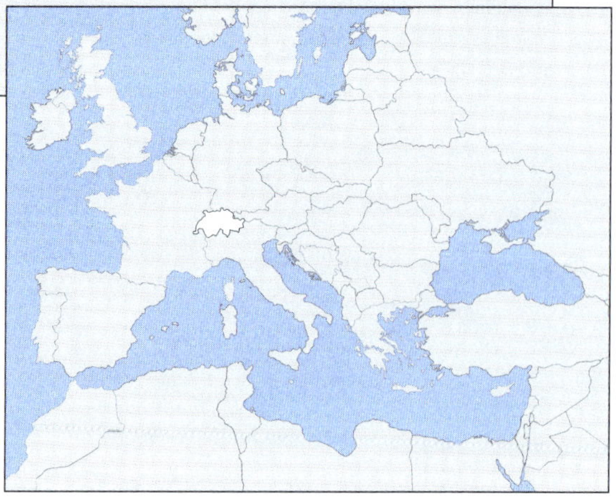

Label the map using terms from the word bank.

WORD BANK

Austria	Rhone River	Germany	France
The Alps	Bern	Rhine River	Liechtenstein
Italy	Vaduz	Geneva	

AUSTRIA

Country: Austria Capital: Vienna Ancient Name: Noricum

Fun Facts: Answers will vary.

Copy the name of the country and its capital three times. Pay close attention to correct spelling.

1. ______________________________

2. ______________________________

3. ______________________________

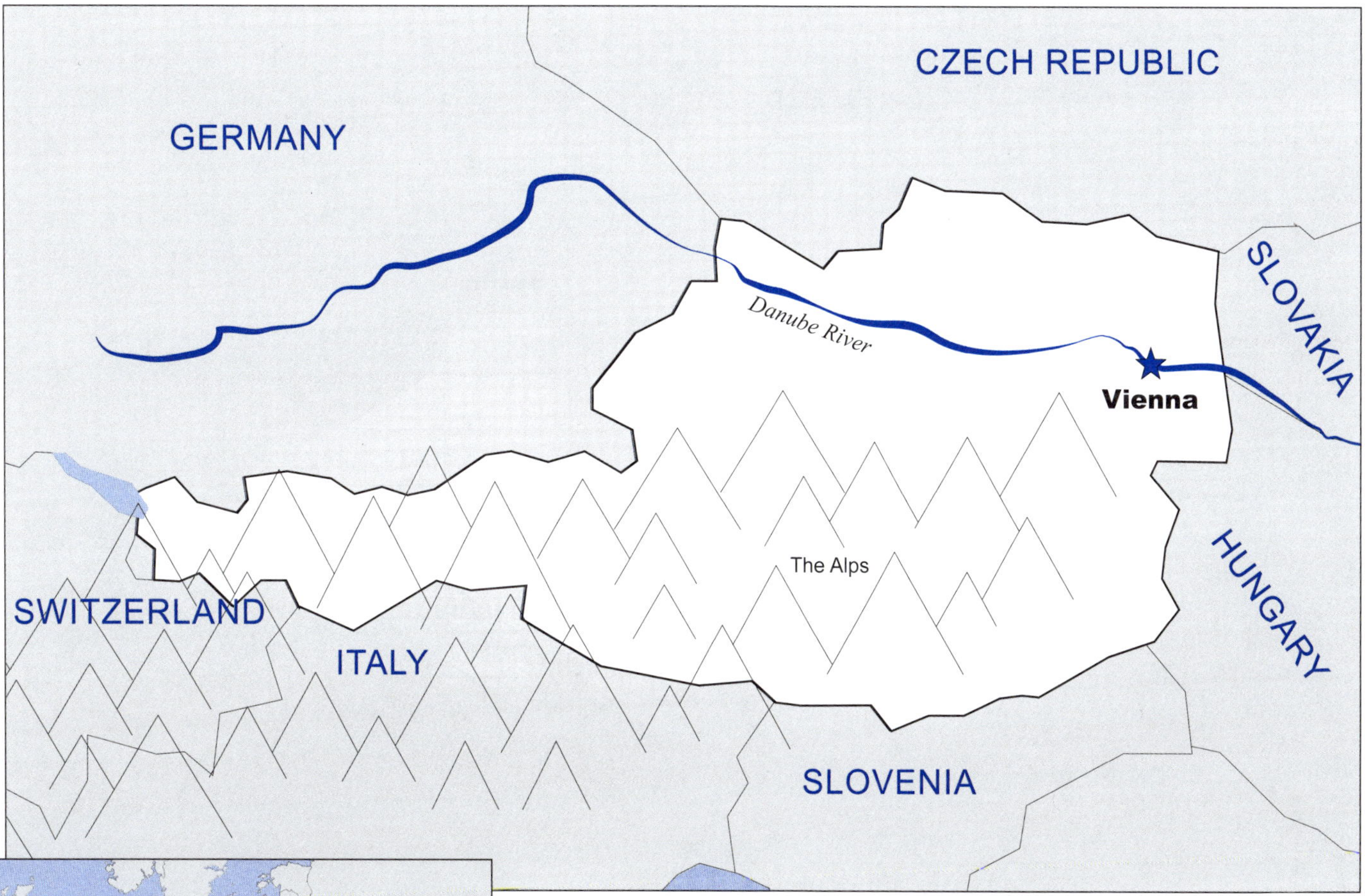

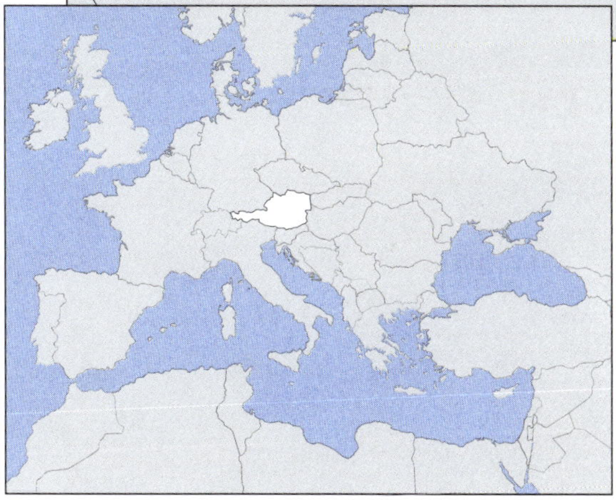

Label the map using terms from the word bank.

WORD BANK

Slovenia	Switzerland	Danube River
Hungary	Slovakia	The Alps
Italy	Germany	
Vienna	Czech Republic	

GERMANY

Country: Germany Capital: Berlin Ancient Name: Germania

Fun Facts: Answers will vary.

Copy the name of the country and its capital three times. Pay close attention to correct spelling.

1. ______________________________
2. ______________________________
3. ______________________________

Label the map using terms from the word bank.

WORD BANK

Czech Republic	France	Frankfurt
Poland	Belgium	Netherlands
North Sea	Munich	Elbe River
Rhine River	Switzerland	Berlin
Luxembourg	Baltic Sea	
Austria	Danube River	

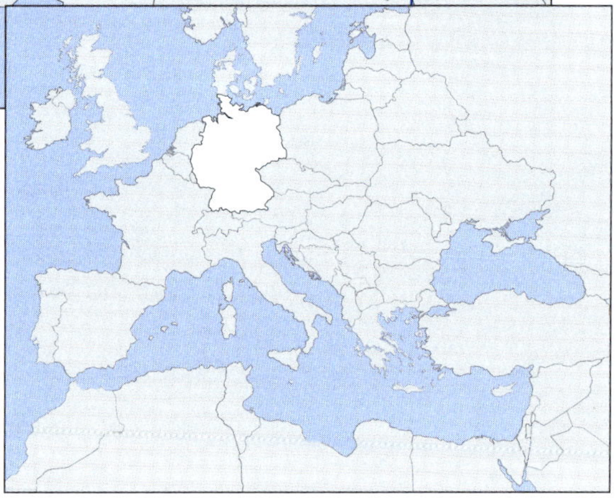

REVIEW

Central Europe

On the map below, label and color each of the countries you have studied.

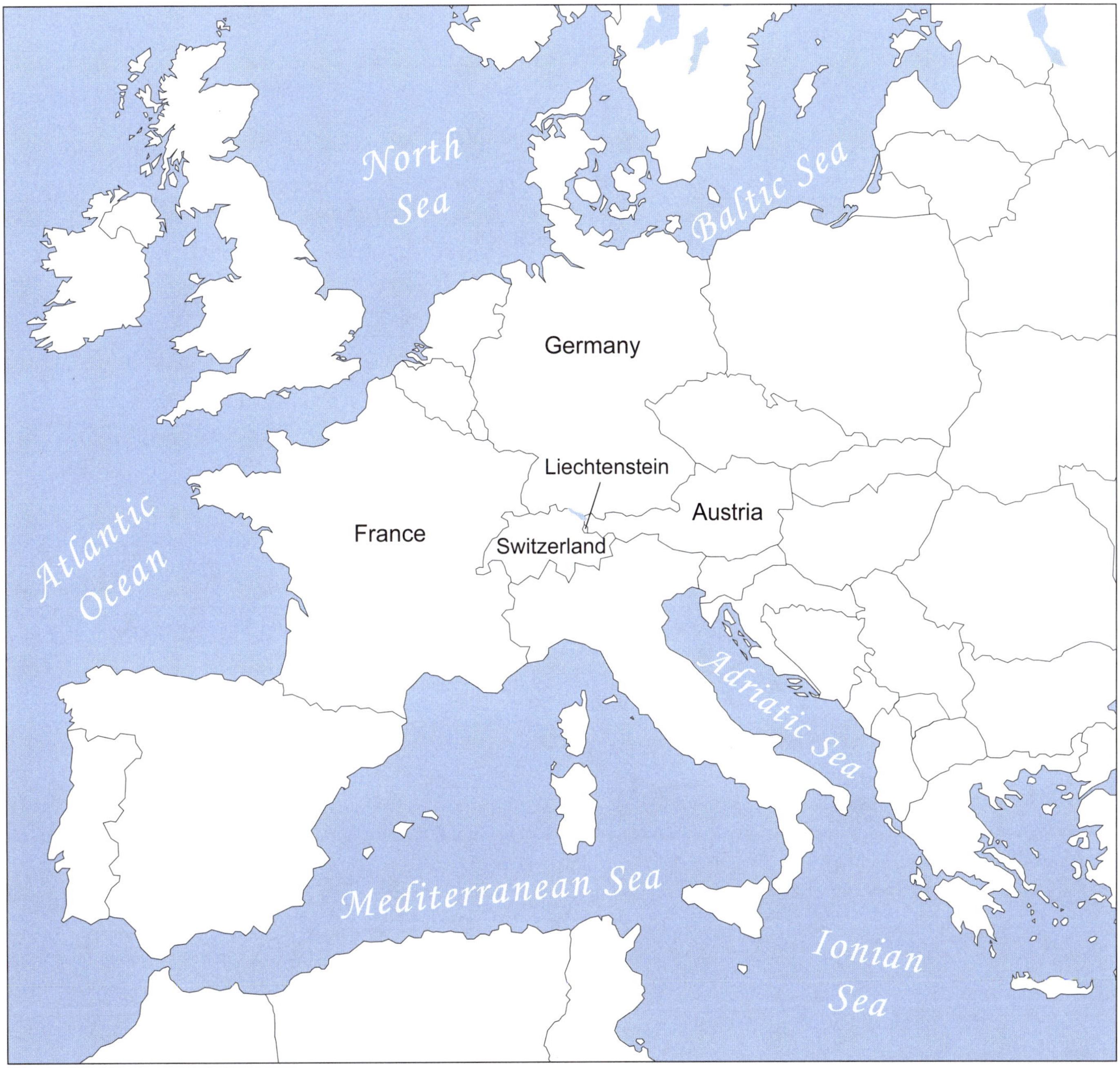

***Note to Teachers*:**
Students should color each of the labeled countries a different color. If time allows, the rest of the countries should be colored the same color, and the bodies of water labeled.

REVIEW

Central Europe

Copy the names of the countries and their capitals below. Pay close attention to correct spelling.

1. Country: France Capital: Paris
2. Country: Switzerland Capital: Bern
3. Country: Liechtenstein Capital: Vaduz
4. Country: Austria Capital: Vienna
5. Country: Germany Capital: Berlin

Use the map below to practice identifying the countries.

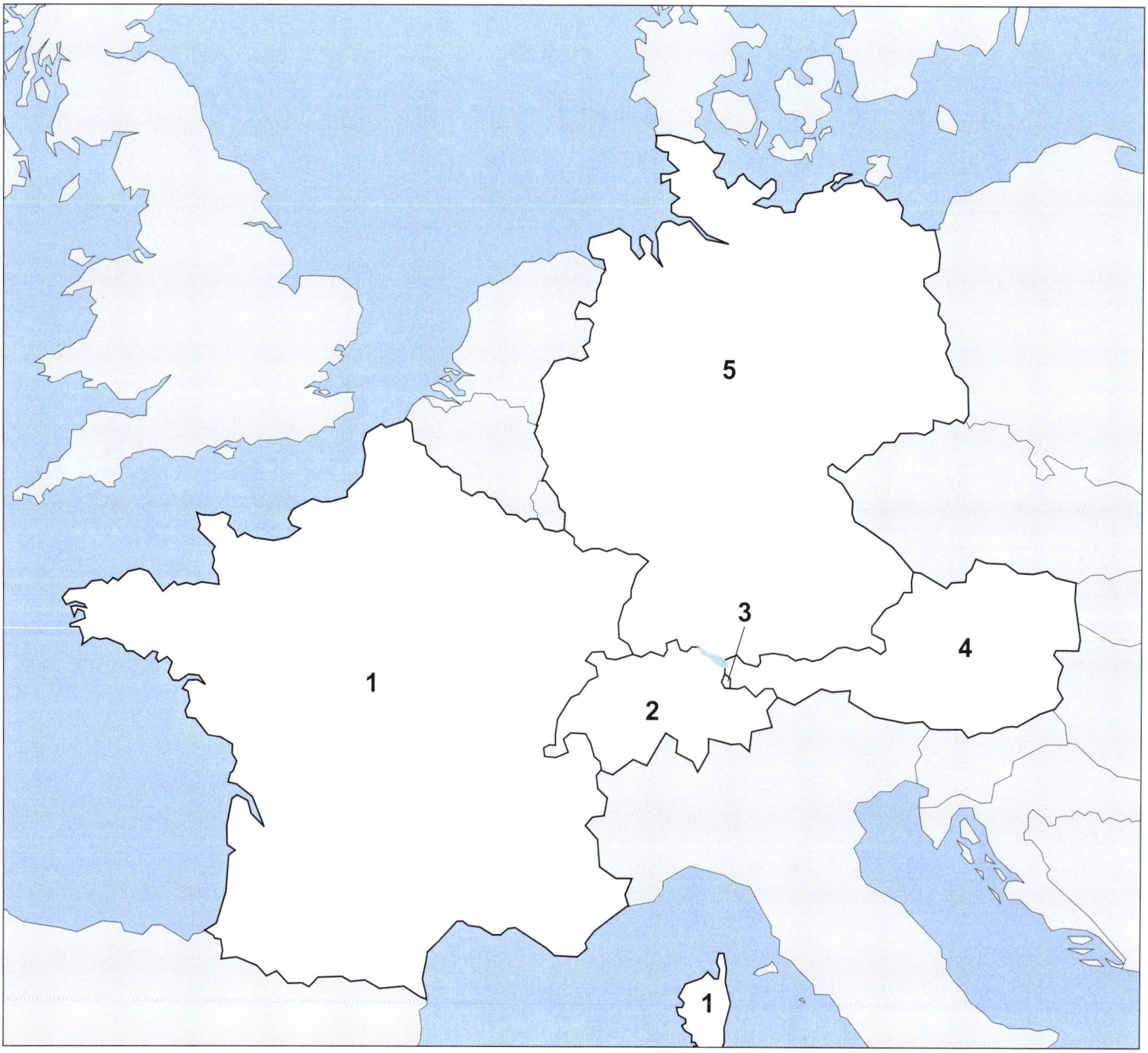

THE BRITISH ISLES

THE BRITISH ISLES

and the Low Countries

Look at the map below. Identify each country.

1. Ireland
2. United Kingdom
3. Belgium
4. Luxembourg
5. Netherlands

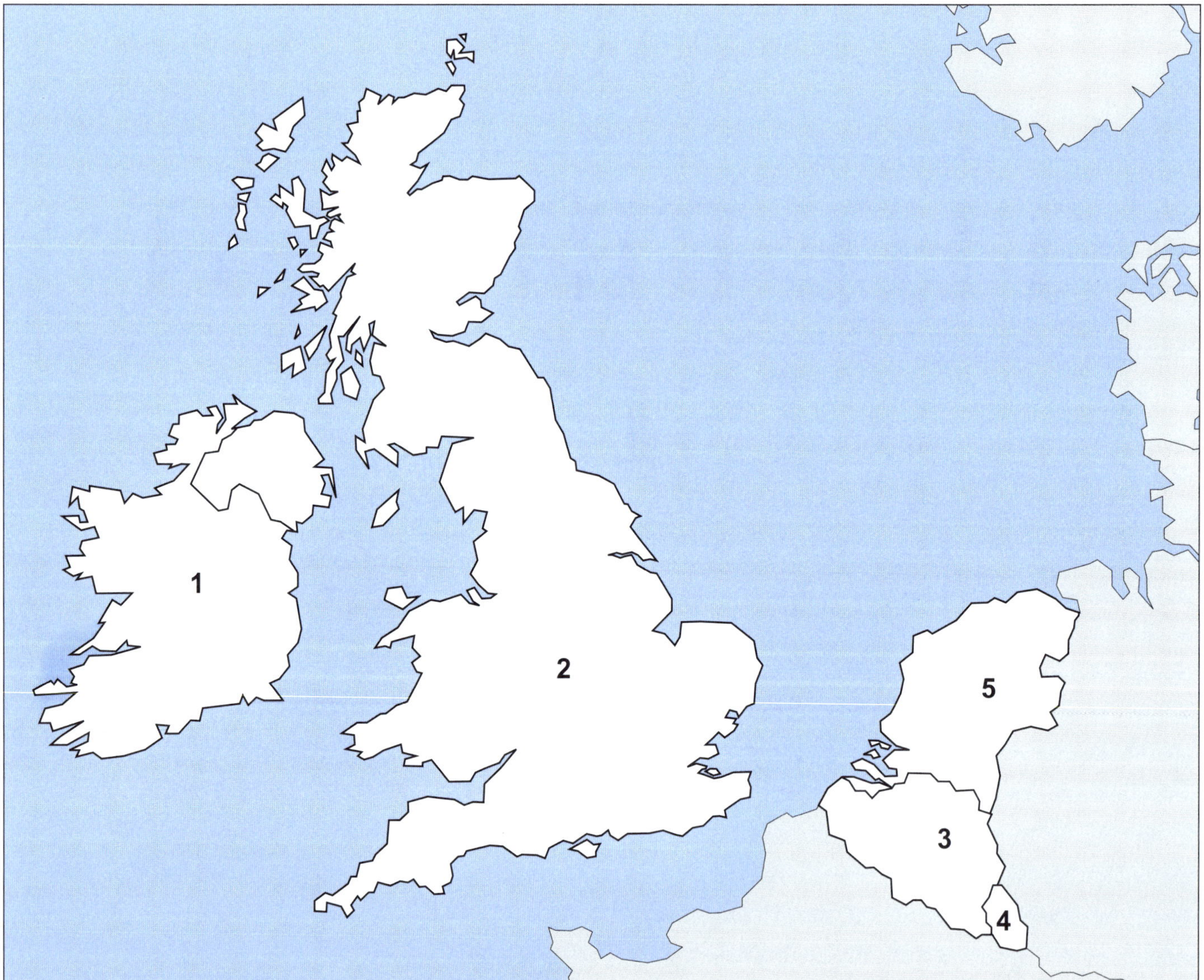

NETHERLANDS

Country: Netherlands Capital: Amsterdam Ancient Name: Land of the Batavians

Fun Facts: Answers will vary.

Copy the name of the country and its capital three times. Pay close attention to correct spelling.

1. ______________________________
2. ______________________________
3. ______________________________

Label the map using terms from the word bank.

WORD BANK

The Hague	Belgium	Amsterdam
Germany	Meuse River	North Sea
England	Rhine River	

BELGIUM & LUXEMBOURG

Country: Belgium Capital: Brussels Ancient Name: Belgica

Country: Luxembourg Capital: Luxembourg City Ancient Name: Belgica

Fun Facts: Answers will vary.

Copy the name of the countries and their capitals three times. Pay close attention to correct spelling.

1. ______________ 1. ______________

2. ______________ 2. ______________

3. ______________ 3. ______________

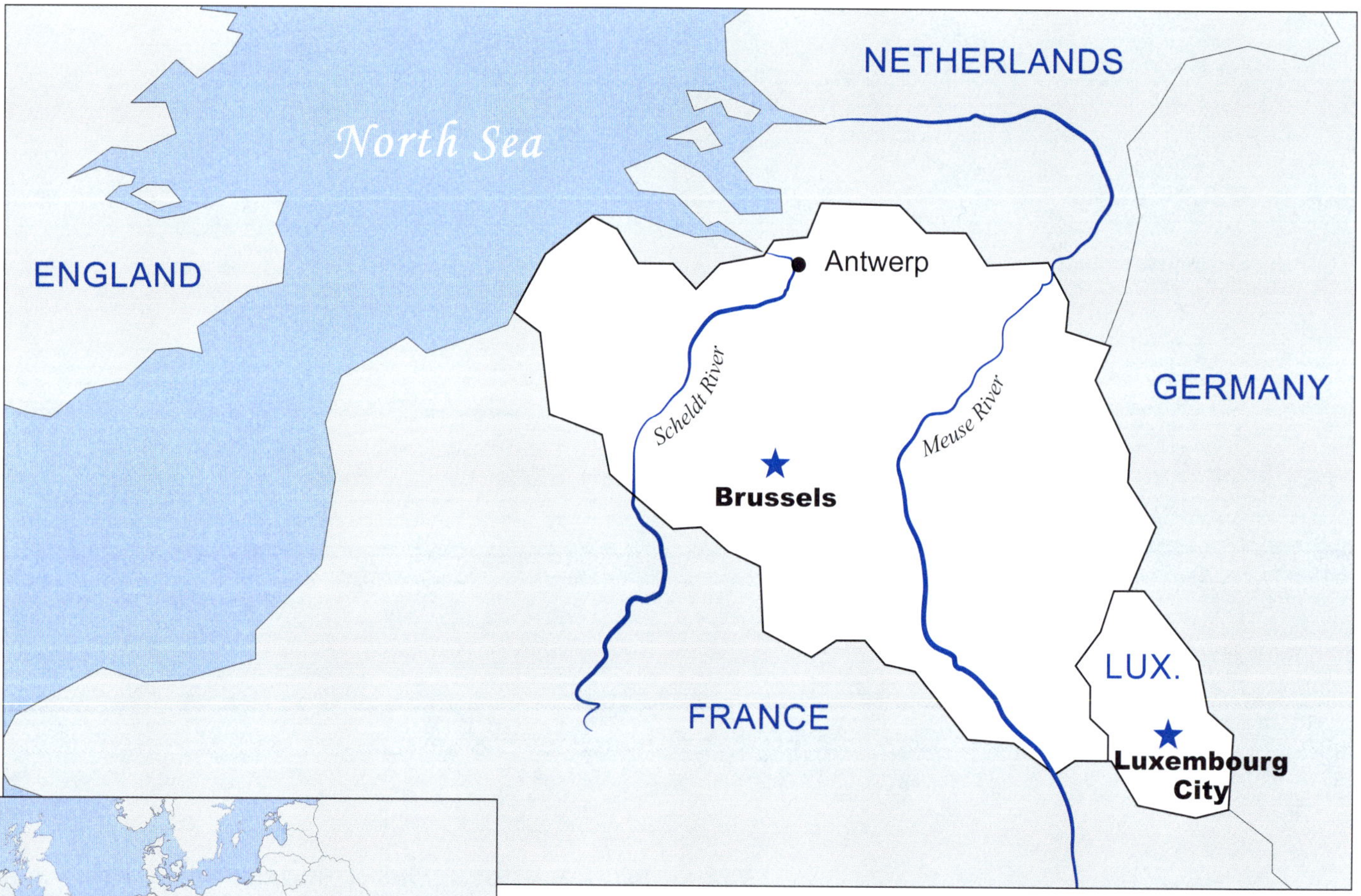

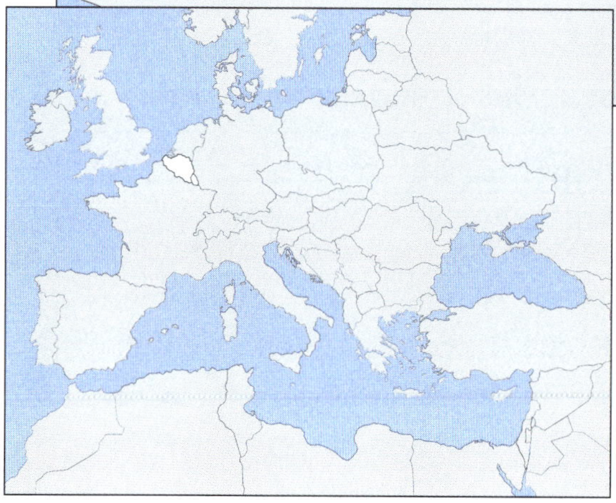

Label the map using terms from the word bank.

WORD BANK

North Sea	Meuse River	England
Brussels	Netherlands	Scheldt River
Germany	Luxembourg	Luxembourg City
France	Antwerp	

UNITED KINGDOM

Country: United Kingdom Capital: London Ancient Name: Britannia

Fun Facts: Answers will vary.

Copy the name of the country and its capital three times. Pay close attention to correct spelling.

1. ______________________________
2. ______________________________
3. ______________________________

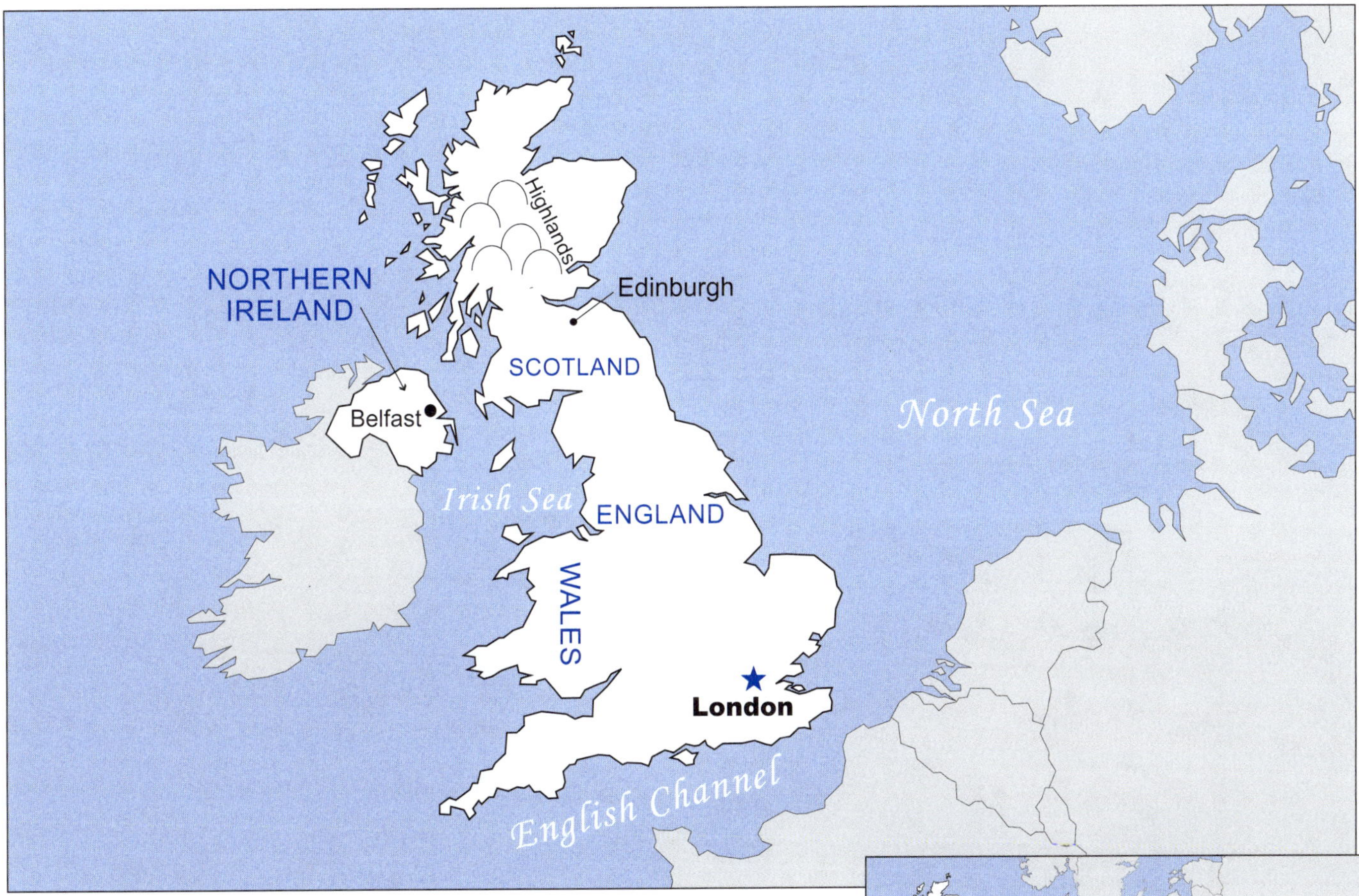

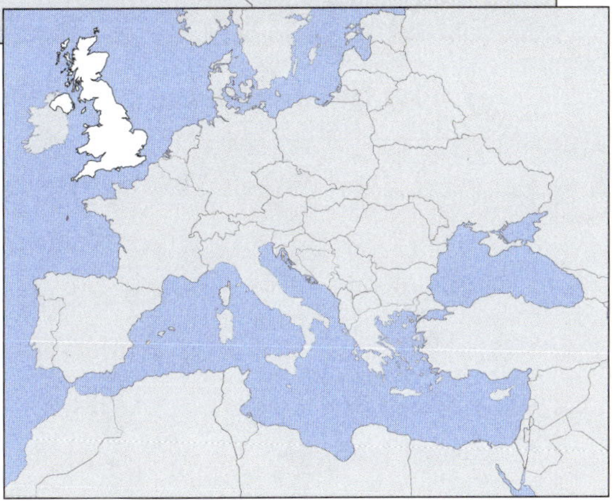

Label the map using terms from the word bank.

WORD BANK

Scotland	Wales	Northern Ireland
Belfast	London	Edinburgh
Irish Sea	English Channel	Highlands
England	North Sea	

IRELAND

Country: Ireland Capital: Dublin Ancient Name: Hibernia

Fun Facts: Answers will vary.

Copy the name of the country and its capital three times. Pay close attention to correct spelling.

1. ______________________________
2. ______________________________
3. ______________________________

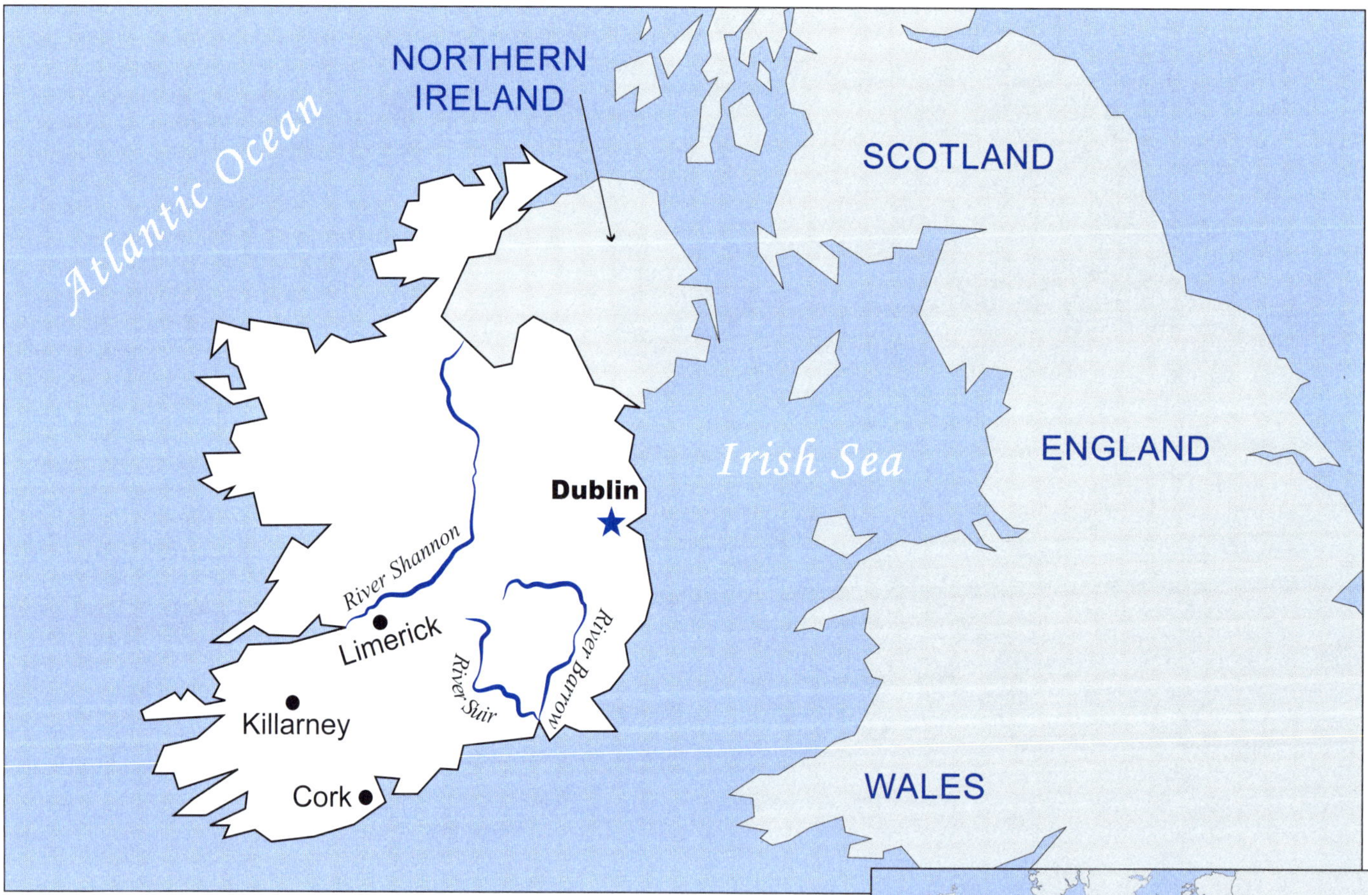

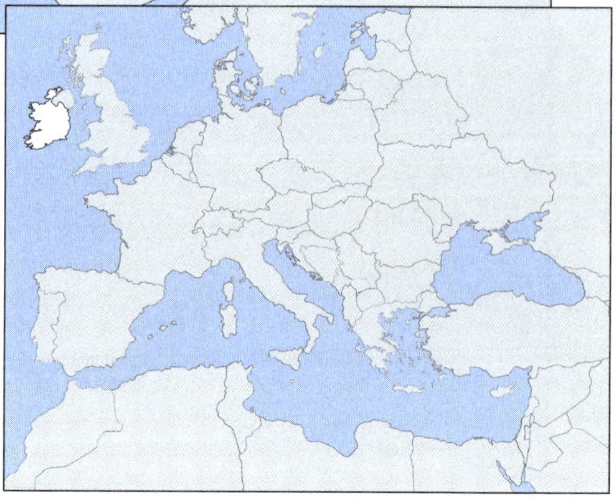

Label the map using terms from the word bank.

WORD BANK		
Irish Sea	River Shannon	Atlantic Ocean
Scotland	River Suir	River Barrow
Wales	Limerick	England
Killarney	Dublin	
Northern Ireland	Cork	

REVIEW

The British Isles & the Low Countries

On the map below, label and color each of the countries you have studied.

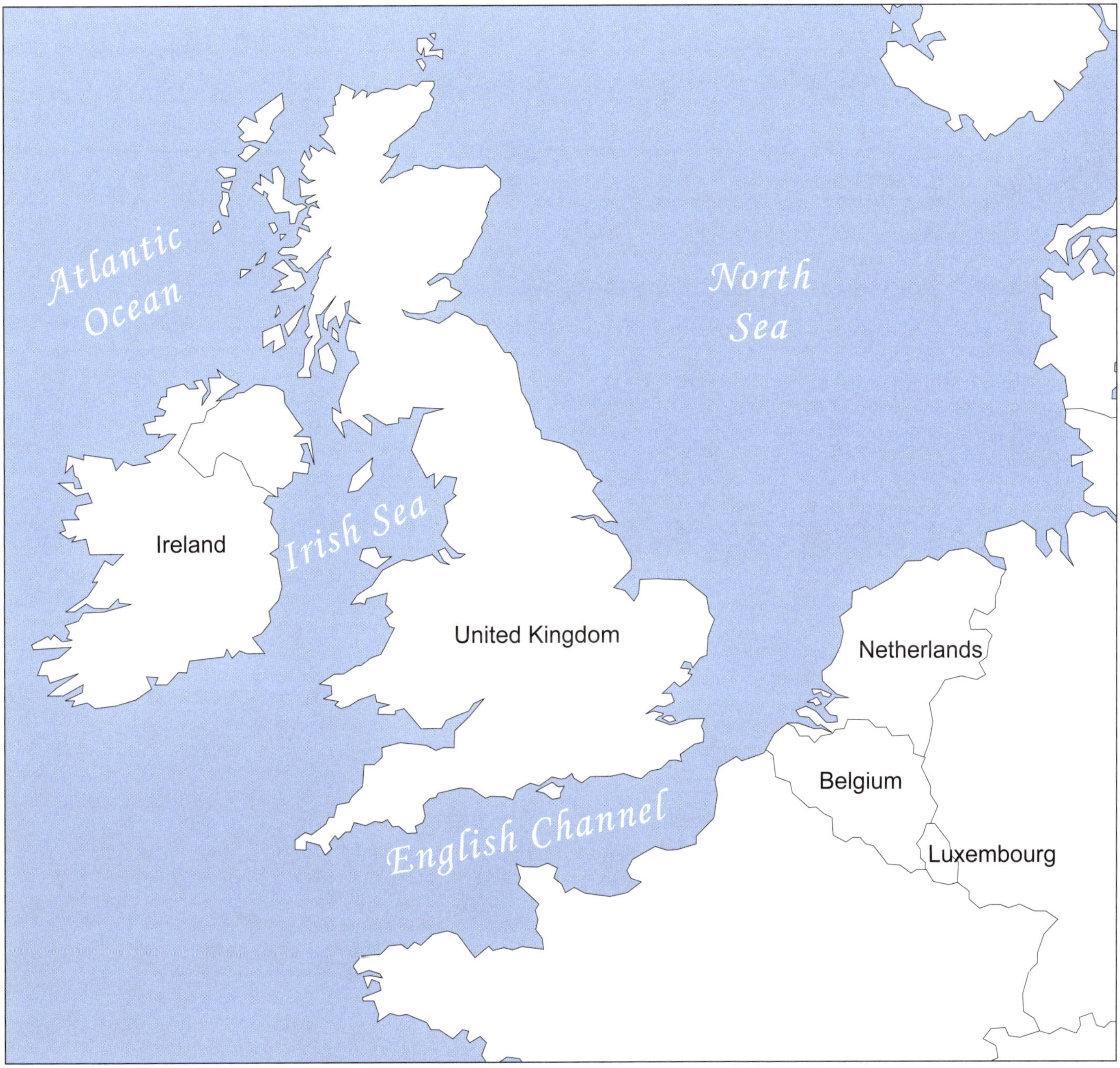

***Note to Teachers*:**
Students should color each of the labeled countries a different color. If time allows, the rest of the countries should be colored the same color, and the bodies of water labeled.

REVIEW

The British Isles & the Low Countries

Copy the names of the countries and their capitals below. Pay close attention to correct spelling.

1. Country: Netherlands Capital: Amsterdam
2. Country: Belgium Capital: Brussels
3. Country: United Kingdom Capital: London
4. Country: Ireland Capital: Dublin
5. Country: Luxembourg Capital: Luxembourg

Use the map below to practice identifying the countries.

REVIEW

Europe Part I

On the map below, label and color each of the countries you have studied.

Note to Teachers:

Students should color each of the labeled countries a different color. If time allows, the rest of the countries should be colored the same color, and the bodies of water labeled.

REVIEW

Europe Part I

Copy the names of the countries and their capitals below. Pay close attention to correct spelling.

1. Country:	Greece	Capital:	Athens
2. Country:	Italy	Capital:	Rome
3. Country:	Spain	Capital:	Madrid
4. Country:	Portugal	Capital:	Lisbon
5. Country:	France	Capital:	Paris
6. Country:	Switzerland	Capital:	Bern
7. Country:	Liechtenstein	Capital:	Vaduz
8. Country:	Austria	Capital:	Vienna
9. Country:	Germany	Capital:	Berlin
10. Country:	Netherlands	Capital:	Amsterdam
11. Country:	Belgium	Capital:	Brussels
12. Country:	Luxembourg	Capital:	Luxembourg
13. Country:	United Kingdom	Capital:	London
14. Country:	Ireland	Capital:	Dublin

Use the map on the next page to practice identifying the countries.

1
2
2
2
3
4
5
5
6
7
8
9
10
11
12
13
14

SCANDINAVIA

SCANDINAVIA

Look at the map below. Identify each country.

1. Iceland
2. Norway
3. Sweden
4. Finland
5. Denmark

NORWAY

Country: Norway Capital: Oslo Ancient Name: The North Way

Fun Facts: Answers will vary.

Copy the name of the country and its capital three times. Pay close attention to correct spelling.

1. ______

2. ______

3. ______

Label the map using terms from the word bank.

WORD BANK

Sweden	Norwegian Sea
Oslo	Arctic Circle
Finland	North Sea
Russia	

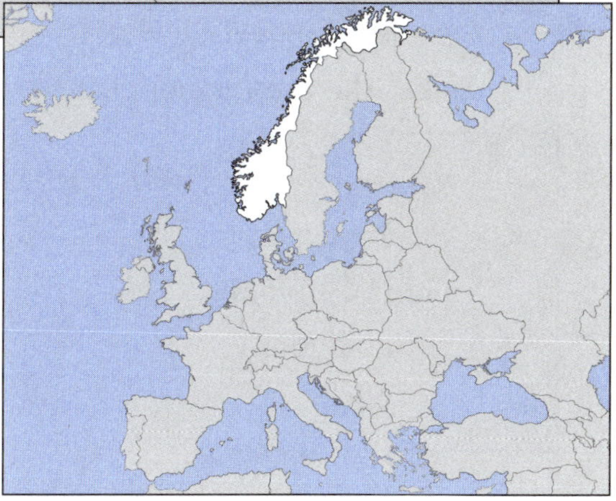

SWEDEN

Country: Sweden Capital: Stockholm Ancient Name: Suiones

Fun Facts: Answers will vary.

Copy the name of the country and its capital three times. Pay close attention to correct spelling.

1. ______________________________

2. ______________________________

3. ______________________________

Label the map using terms from the word bank.

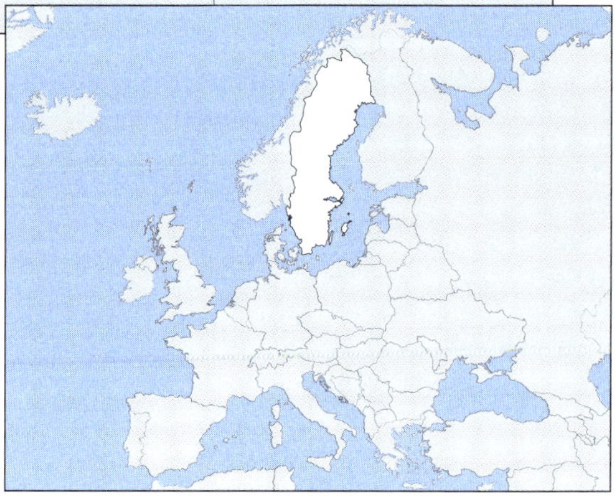

WORD BANK	
Finland	North Sea
Gulf of Bothnia	Arctic Circle
Stockholm	
Norway	

DENMARK

Country: Denmark Capital: Copenhagen Ancient Name: Teutones, Ambrones, and Cimbri

Fun Facts: Answers will vary.

Copy the name of the country and its capital three times. Pay close attention to correct spelling.

1.
2.
3.

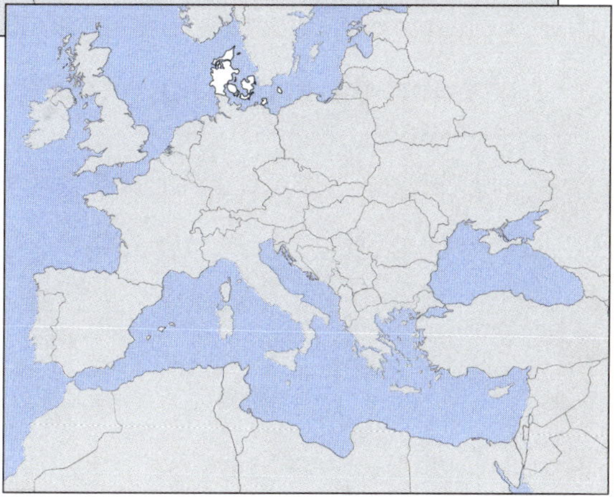

Label the map using terms from the word bank.

WORD BANK

Jutland	Germany
Funen	North Sea
Zealand	Sweden
Copenhagen	Norway
Baltic Sea	

ICELAND

Country: Iceland Capital: Reykjavik Ancient Name: Land of Fire and Ice

Fun Facts: Answers will vary.

Copy the name of the country and its capital three times. Pay close attention to correct spelling.

1. ____________________

2. ____________________

3. ____________________

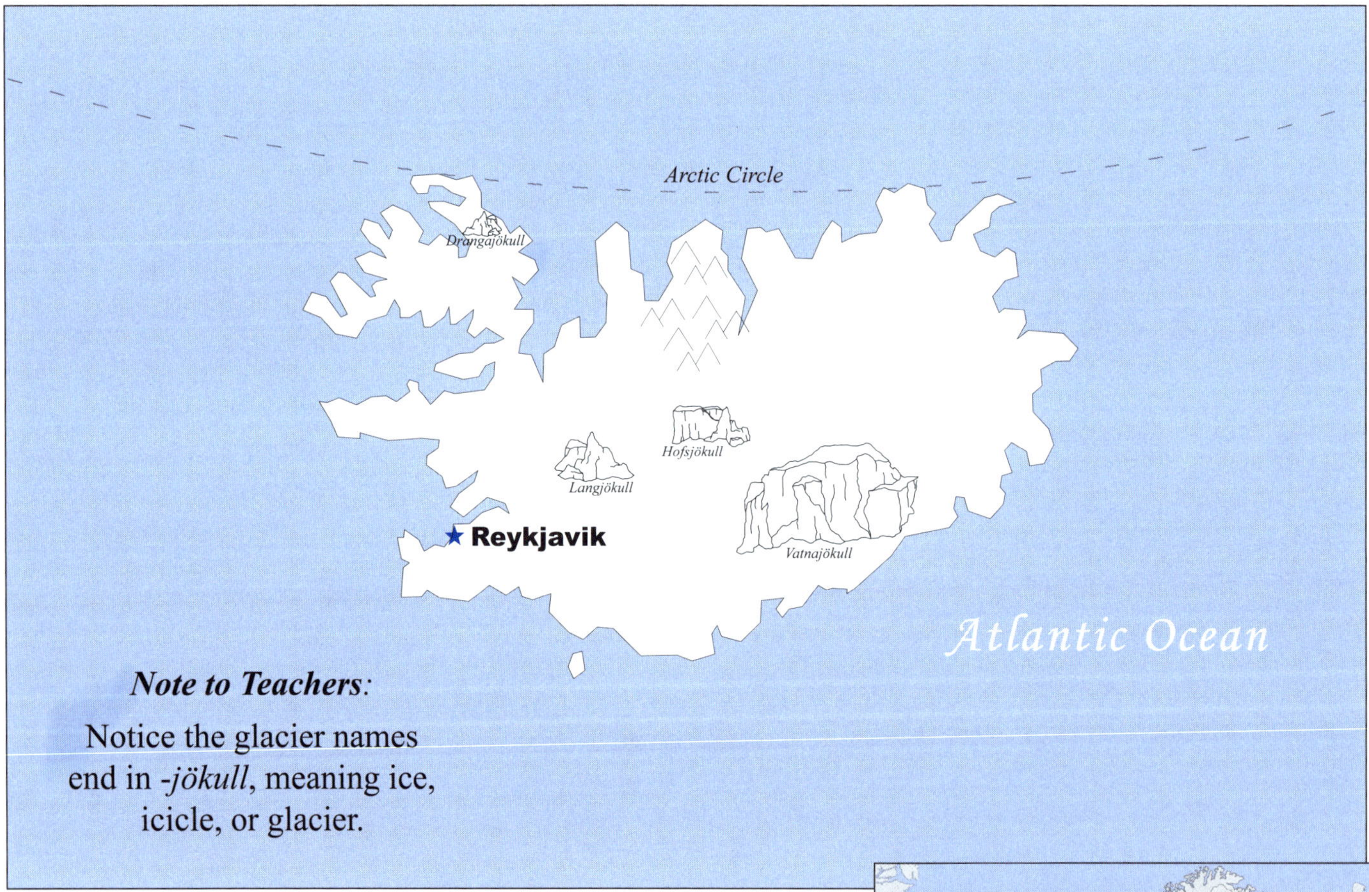

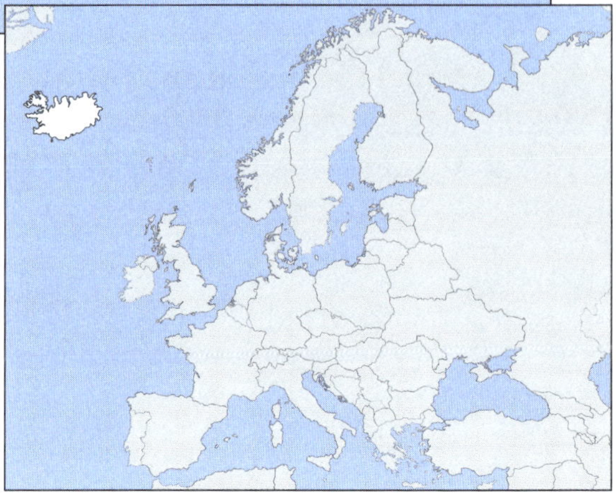

Label the map using terms from the word bank.

WORD BANK		
Reykjavik	Atlantic Ocean	Arctic Circle

FINLAND

Country: Finland Capital: Helsinki Ancient Name: N/A

Fun Facts: Answers will vary.

Copy the name of the country and its capital three times. Pay close attention to correct spelling.

1. ______________________________
2. ______________________________
3. ______________________________

Label the map using terms from the word bank.

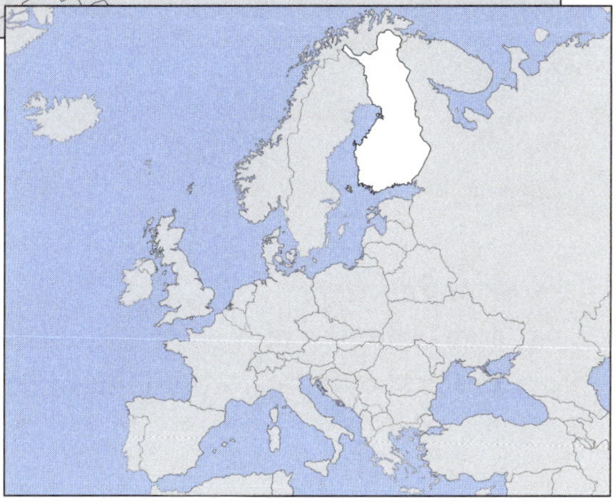

WORD BANK	
Arctic Circle	Helsinki
Sweden	Russia
Baltic Sea	Norway

REVIEW

Scandinavia

On the map below, label and color each of the countries you have studied.

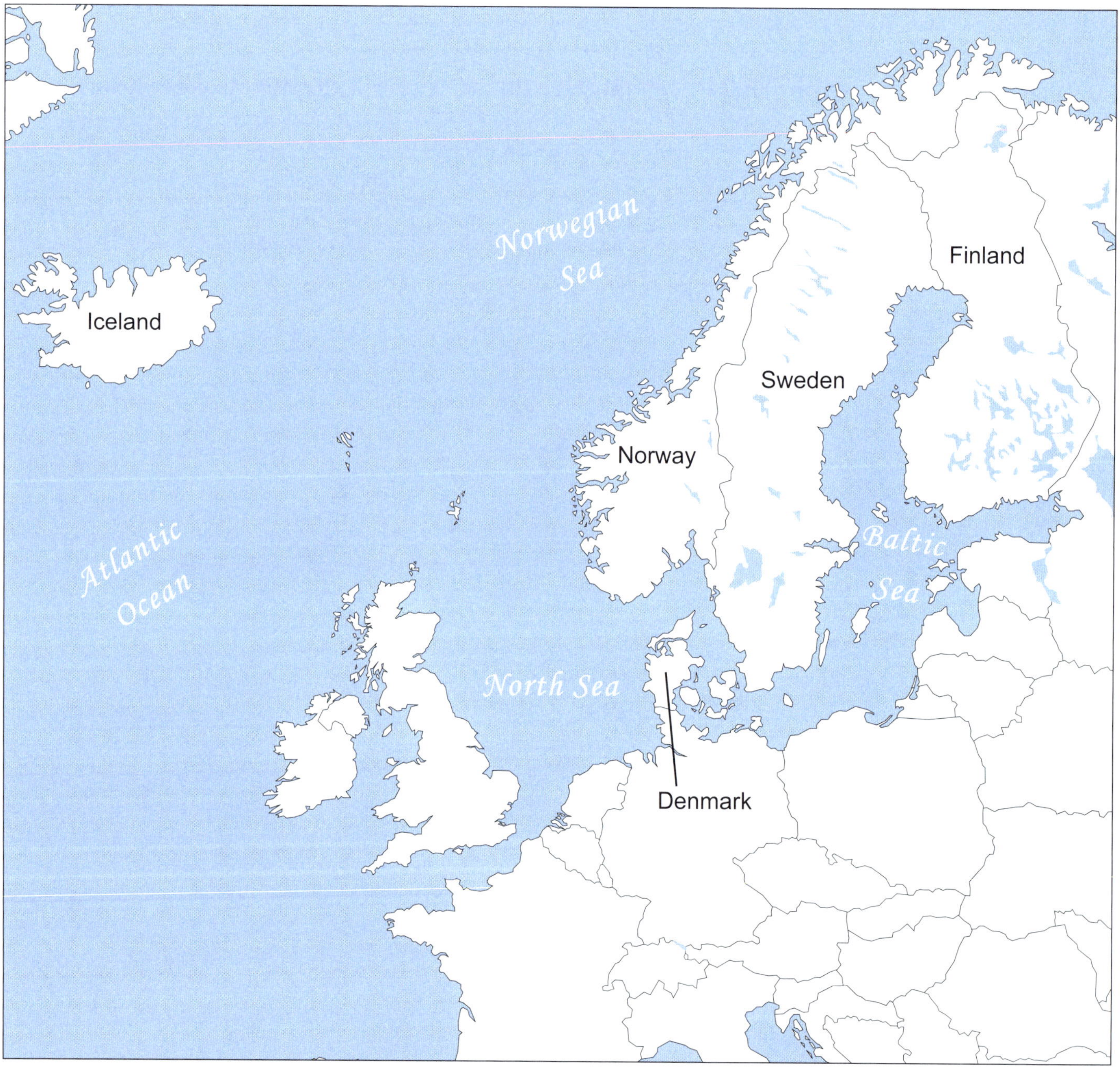

Note to Teachers:
Students should color each of the labeled countries a different color. If time allows, the rest of the countries should be colored the same color, and the bodies of water labeled.

REVIEW

Scandinavia

Copy the names of the countries and their capitals below. Pay close attention to correct spelling.

1. Country: Norway — Capital: Oslo
2. Country: Sweden — Capital: Stockholm
3. Country: Denmark — Capital: Copenhagen
4. Country: Iceland — Capital: Reykjavik
5. Country: Finland — Capital: Helsinki

Use the map below to practice identifying the countries.

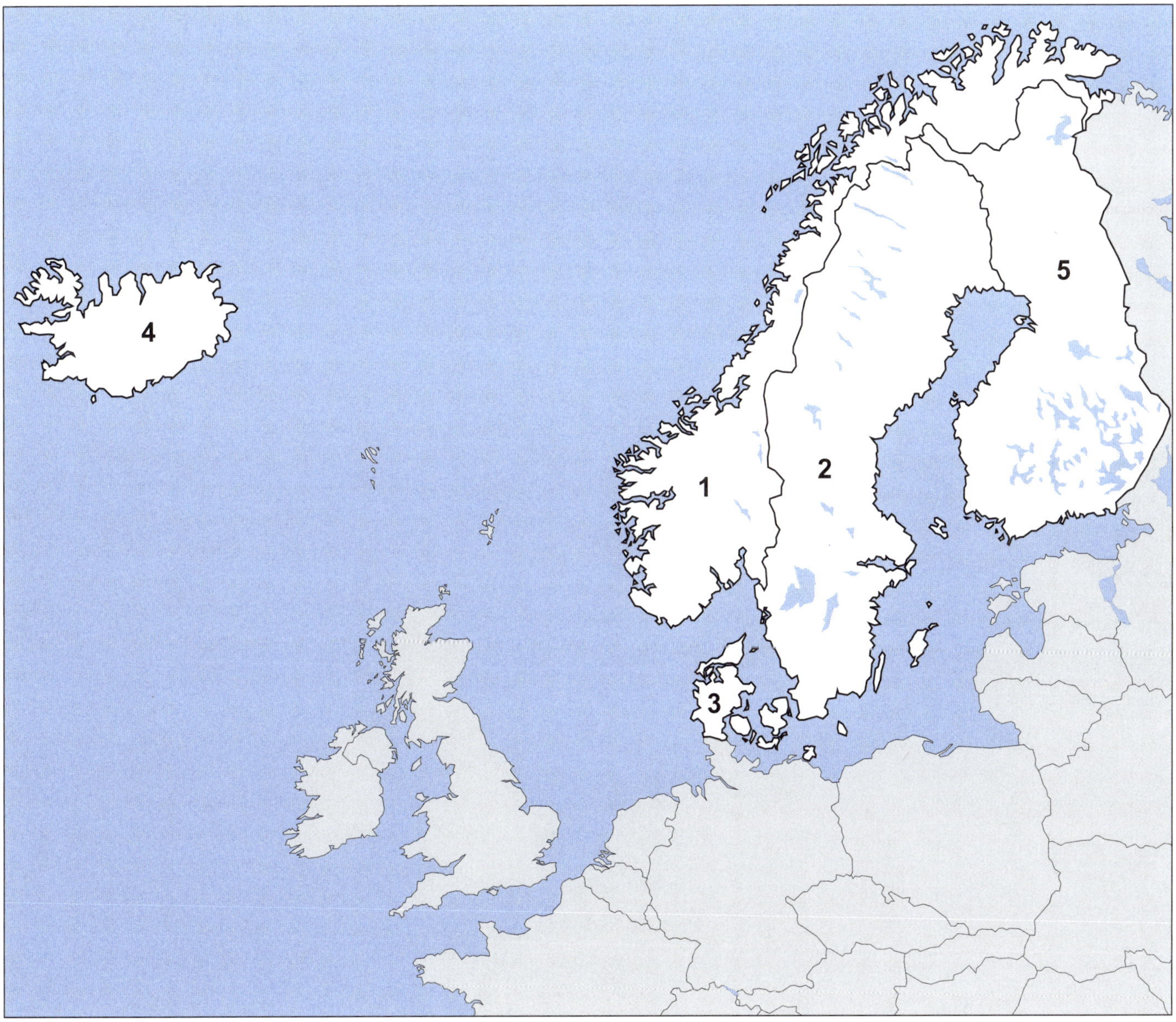

EASTERN EUROPE

EASTERN EUROPE

Look at the map below. Identify each country.

1. Hungary
2. The Balkans
3. Bulgaria
4. Romania
5. Ukraine
6. Belarus
7. Russia
8. The Baltic States
9. Poland
10. Czech Republic
11. Albania
12. Slovakia
13. Moldova

RUSSIA

Country: Russia Capital: Moscow Ancient Name: Scythia

Fun Facts: Answers will vary.

Copy the name of the country and its capital three times. Pay close attention to correct spelling.

1. ______

2. ______

3. ______

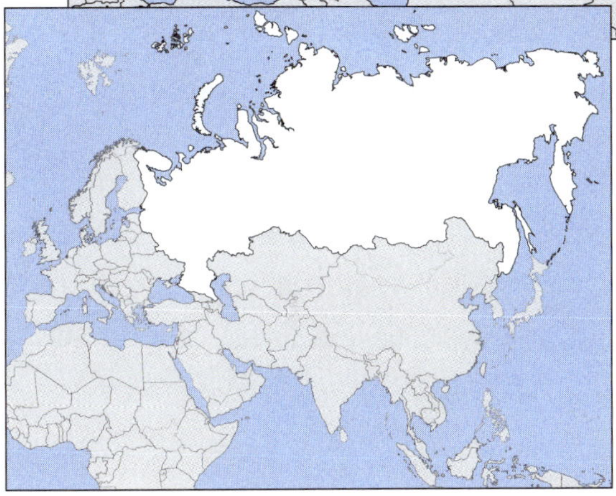

Label the map using terms from the word bank.

WORD BANK

Pacific Ocean	Arctic Ocean	Volga River
Siberia	St. Petersburg	Arctic Circle
Ural Mountains	Moscow	

ESTONIA

Baltic State

Country: Estonia Capital: Tallinn Ancient Name: Balts

Fun Facts: Answers will vary.

Copy the name of the country and its capital three times. Pay close attention to correct spelling.

1. ______________________________

2. ______________________________

3. ______________________________

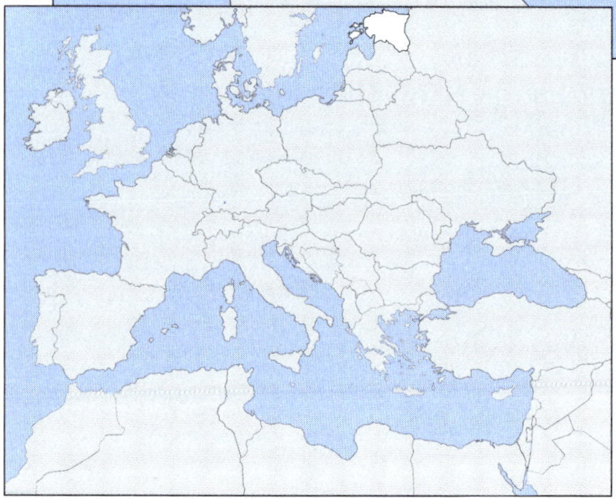

Label the map using terms from the word bank.

WORD BANK	
Russia	Tallinn
Latvia	Baltic Sea

LATVIA

Baltic State

Country: Latvia Capital: Riga Ancient Name: Balts

Fun Facts: Answers will vary.

Copy the name of the country and its capital three times. Pay close attention to correct spelling.

1. ______________________
2. ______________________
3. ______________________

Label the map using terms from the word bank.

WORD BANK

Riga	Estonia
Lithuania	Belarus
Baltic Sea	Daugava River
Russia	

LITHUANIA

Baltic State

Country: Lithuania Capital: Vilnius Ancient Name: Balts

Fun Facts: Answers will vary.

Copy the name of the country and its capital three times. Pay close attention to correct spelling.

1. ____________________

2. ____________________

3. ____________________

Label the map using terms from the word bank.

WORD BANK		
Vilnius	Poland	Latvia
Belarus	Nemunas River	

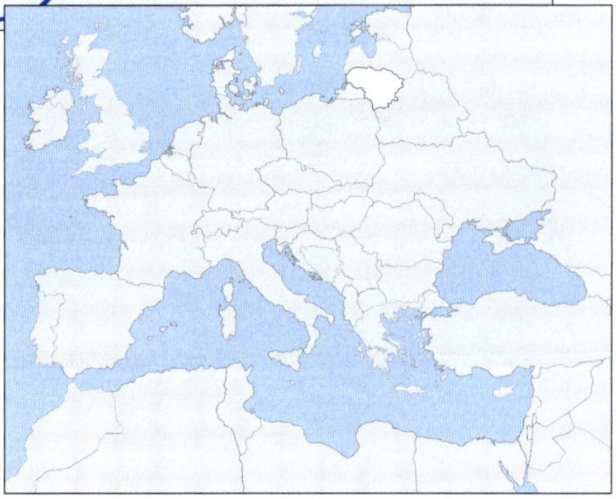

BELARUS

Country: Belarus Capital: Minsk Ancient Name: N/A

Fun Facts: Answers will vary.

Copy the name of the country and its capital three times. Pay close attention to correct spelling.

1. ______

2. ______

3. ______

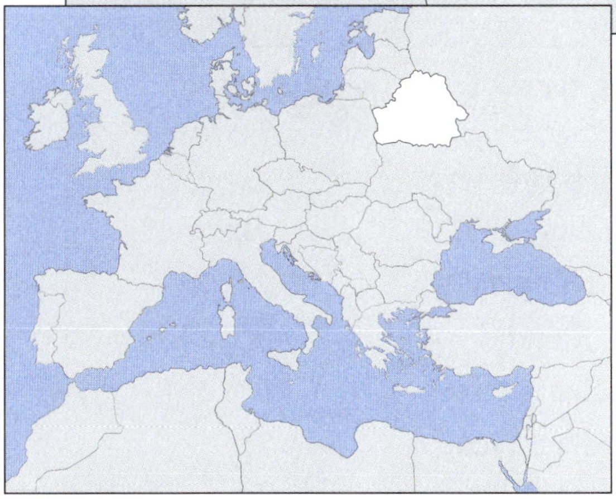

Label the map using terms from the word bank.

WORD BANK

Neman River	Dnieper River	Poland
Ukraine	Latvia	Pripyat River
Russia	Lithuania	Minsk

UKRAINE

Country: Ukraine Capital: Kyiv Ancient Name: N/A

Fun Facts: Answers will vary.

Copy the name of the country and its capital three times. Pay close attention to correct spelling.

1. ______________________________
2. ______________________________
3. ______________________________

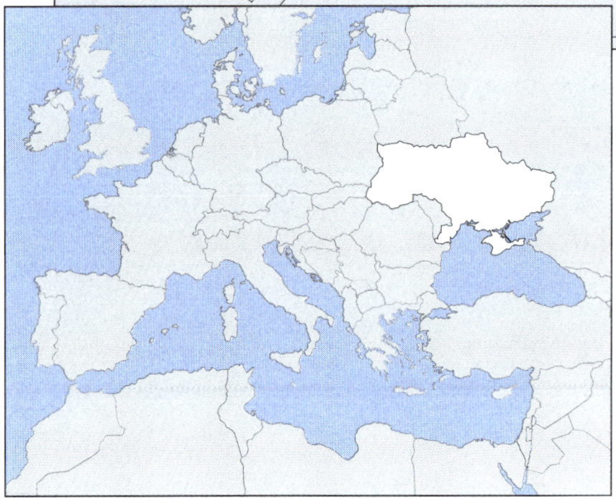

Label the map using terms from the word bank.

WORD BANK

Slovakia	Chernobyl	Belarus
Sea of Azov	Hungary	Kyiv
Romania	Poland	Pripyat River
Moldova	Dnieper River	
Russia	Black Sea	

POLAND

Country: Poland Capital: Warsaw Ancient Name: Celtic, Germanic, and Baltic tribes

Fun Facts: Answers will vary.

Copy the name of the country and its capital three times. Pay close attention to correct spelling.

1. ______________________________
2. ______________________________
3. ______________________________

Label the map using terms from the word bank.

WORD BANK		
Belarus	Baltic Sea	Vistula River
Warsaw	Germany	Ukraine
Slovakia	Oder River	
Czech Republic	Lithuania	

REVIEW

Eastern Europe I

Copy the names of the countries and their capitals below. Pay close attention to correct spelling.

1. Country: Russia Capital: Moscow
2. Country: Estonia Capital: Tallinn
3. Country: Latvia Capital: Riga
4. Country: Lithuania Capital: Vilnius
5. Country: Belarus Capital: Minsk
6. Country: Ukraine Capital: Kyiv
7. Country: Poland Capital: Warsaw

Use the map below to practice identifying the countries.

REVIEW

Eastern Europe I

On the map below, label and color each of the countries you have studied.

Note to Teachers:
Students should color each of the labeled countries a different color. If time allows, the rest of the countries should be colored the same color, and the bodies of water labeled.

THE CZECH REPUBLIC

Country: Czech Republic Capital: Prague Ancient Name: Land of the Marcomanni & Quadi

Fun Facts: Answers will vary.

Copy the name of the country and its capital three times. Pay close attention to correct spelling.

1. ______________________________

2. ______________________________

3. ______________________________

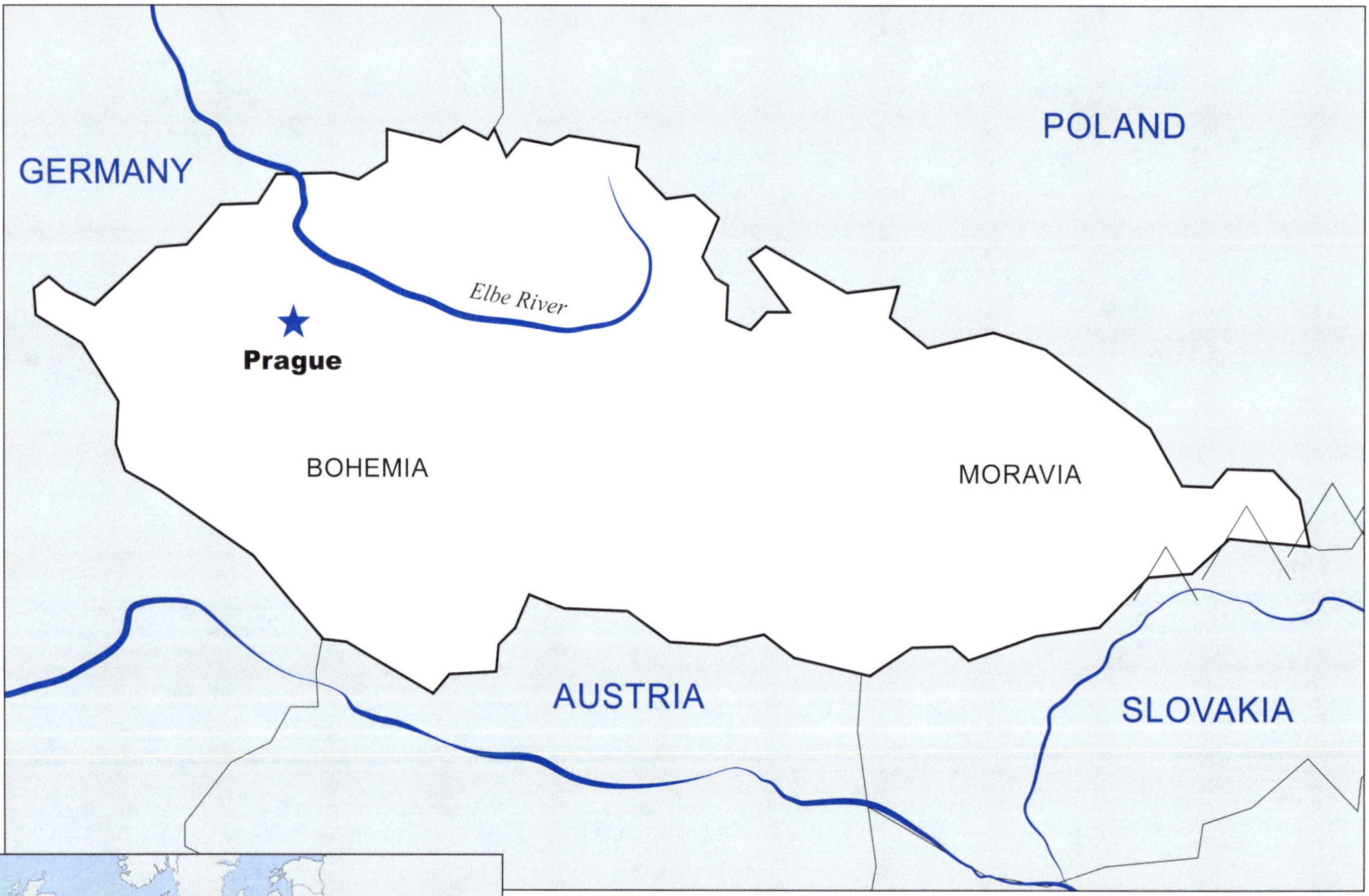

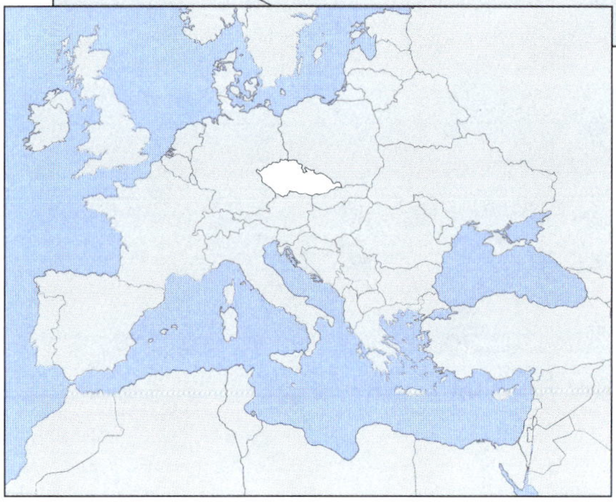

Label the map using terms from the word bank.

WORD BANK		
Moravia	Bohemia	Poland
Slovakia	Prague	Germany
Austria	Elbe River	

SLOVAKIA

Country: Slovakia Capital: Bratislava Ancient Name: Land of the Marcomanni & Quadi

Fun Facts: Answers will vary.

Copy the name of the country and its capital three times. Pay close attention to correct spelling.

1. ______
2. ______
3. ______

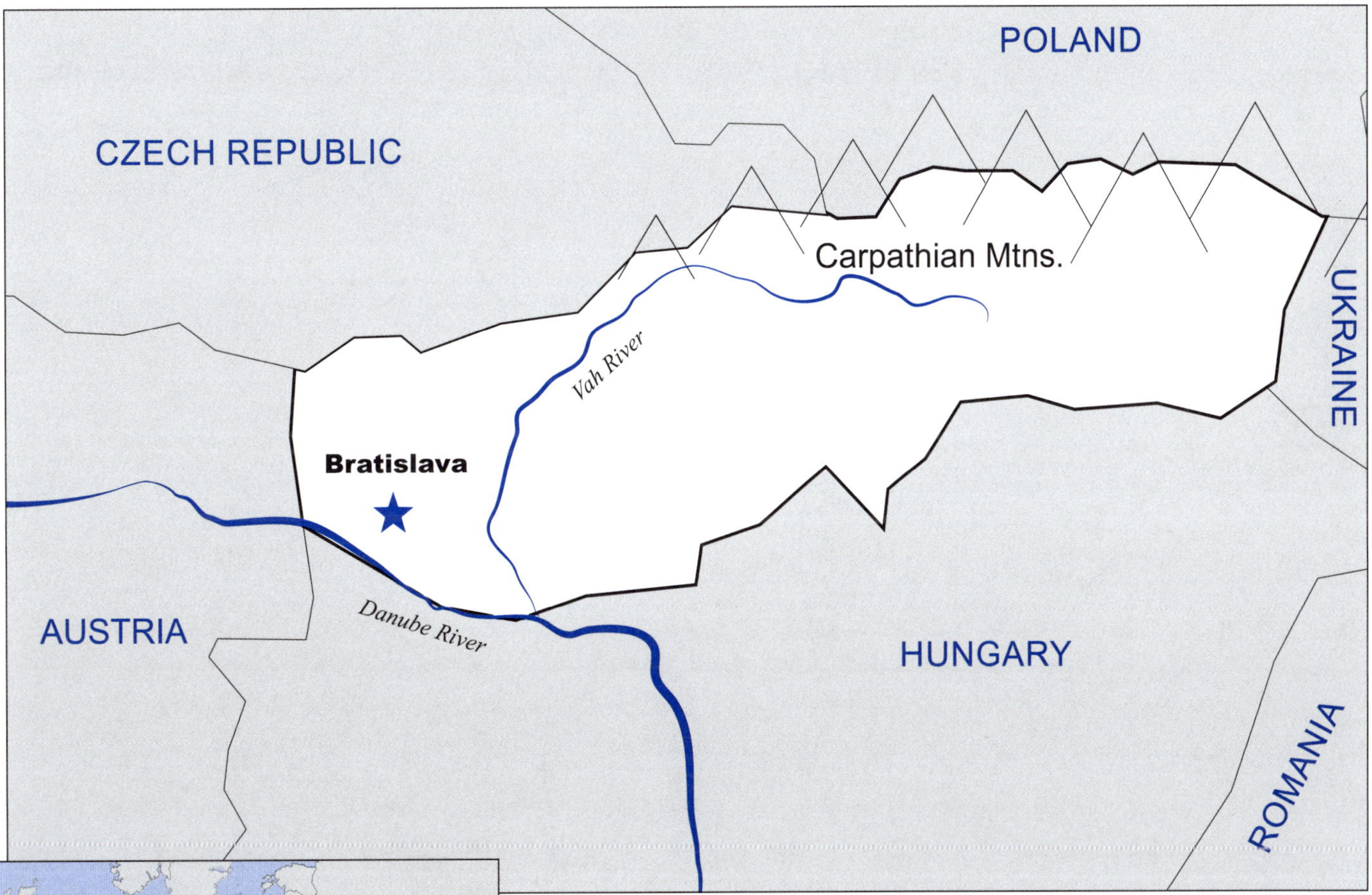

Label the map using terms from the word bank.

WORD BANK

Vah River	Austria	Czech Republic
Hungary	Poland	Bratislava
Romania	Danube River	Ukraine

HUNGARY

Country: Hungary Capital: Budapest Ancient Name: Pannonia

Fun Facts: Answers will vary.

Copy the name of the country and its capital three times. Pay close attention to correct spelling.

1. ______________________________
2. ______________________________
3. ______________________________

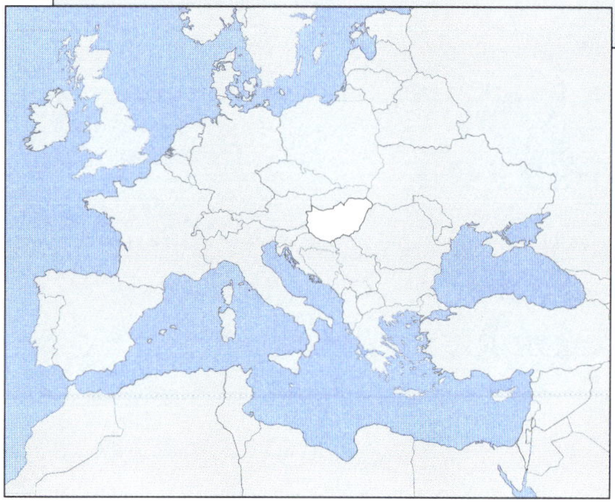

Label the map using terms from the word bank.

WORD BANK

Romania	Slovenia	Tisza River
Serbia	Austria	Ukraine
Slovakia	Budapest	
Danube River	Croatia	

ROMANIA & MOLDOVA

Country: Romania Capital: Bucharest Ancient Name: Dacia

Country: Moldova Capital: Chisinau Ancient Name: Dacia

Fun Facts: Answers will vary.

Copy the name of the countries and their capitals three times. Pay close attention to correct spelling.

1. ______	1. ______
2. ______	2. ______
3. ______	3. ______

Label the map using terms from the word bank.

WORD BANK

Danube River	Moldova	Ukraine
Bulgaria	Hungary	Bucharest
Serbia	Transylvanian Alps	Slovakia
Black Sea	Chisinau	

BULGARIA

Country: Bulgaria Capital: Sofia Ancient Name: Thrace

Fun Facts: Answers will vary.

Copy the name of the country and its capital three times. Pay close attention to correct spelling.

1. ____________________
2. ____________________
3. ____________________

Label the map using terms from the word bank.

WORD BANK

Sofia	Turkey	Danube River
Greece	Black Sea	Serbia
North Macedonia	Romania	Balkan Mountains

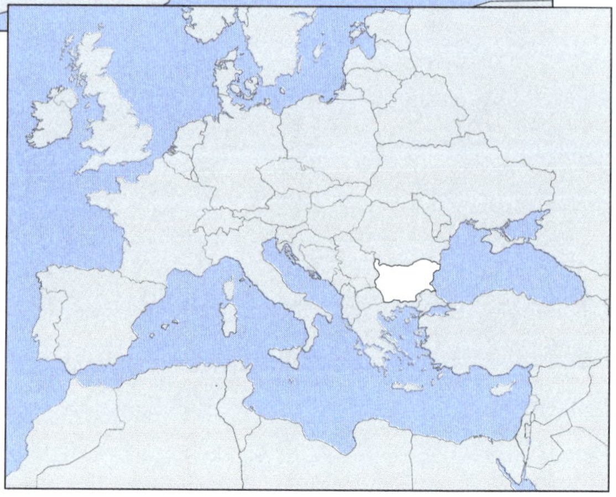

ALBANIA

Country: Albania Capital: Tirana Ancient Name: Epirus Nova

Fun Facts: Answers will vary.

Copy the name of the country and its capital three times. Pay close attention to correct spelling.

1. ____________________

2. ____________________

3. ____________________

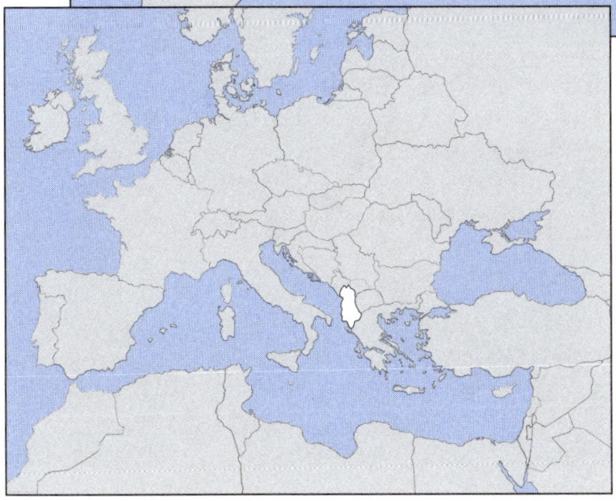

Label the map using terms from the word bank.

WORD BANK

Ionian Sea	Kosovo
Greece	North Macedonia
Tirana	Adriatic Sea
Montenegro	

THE BALKANS

Ancient Name: Illyricum

Fun Facts: Answers will vary.

Copy the names of the countries and their capitals below. Pay attention to correct spelling.

1. Country: Croatia — Capital: Zagreb
2. Country: Bosnia & Herzegovina — Capital: Sarajevo
3. Country: Montenegro — Capital: Podgorica
4. Country: North Macedonia — Capital: Skopje
5. Country: Kosovo — Capital: Pristina
6. Country: Serbia — Capital: Belgrade
7. Country: Slovenia — Capital: Ljubljana

On the map to the right, use the numbers from above to label the countries.

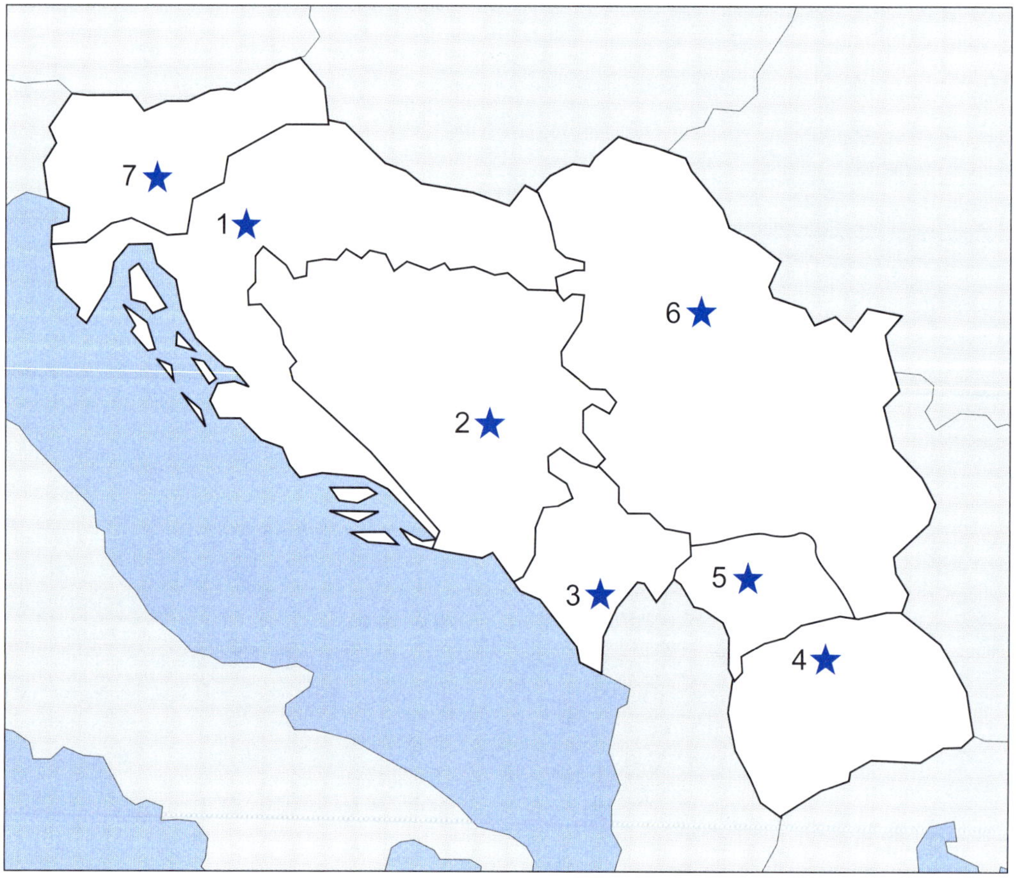

REVIEW

Eastern Europe II

On the map below, label and color each of the countries you have studied.

***Note to Teachers*:**
Students should color each of the labeled countries a different color. If time allows, the rest of the countries should be colored the same color, and the bodies of water labeled.

REVIEW

Eastern Europe II

Copy the names of the countries and their capitals below. Pay close attention to correct spelling.

1. Country: Czech Republic Capital: Prague
2. Country: Slovakia Capital: Bratislava
3. Country: Hungary Capital: Budapest
4. Country: Romania Capital: Bucharest
5. Country: Bulgaria Capital: Sofia
6. Country: Albania Capital: Tirana
7. Country: Moldova Capital: Chisinau
8. Country: Croatia Capital: Zagreb
9. Country: Bosnia & Herzegovina Capital: Sarajevo
10. Country: Montenegro Capital: Podgorica
11. Country: North Macedonia Capital: Skopje
12. Country: Kosovo Capital: Pristina
13. Country: Serbia Capital: Belgrade
14. Country: Slovenia Capital: Ljubljana

Use the map below to practice identifying the countries.

REVIEW

Scandinavia & Eastern Europe

On the map below, color each of the following countries.

Norway	black	The Baltic States	bright red	Hungary	light blue
Sweden	dark brown	Belarus	dark red	Romania	dark blue
Denmark	light brown	Ukraine	orange	Bulgaria	dark purple
Iceland	peach/tan	Poland	yellow	Moldova	light purple
Finland	gold	Czech Republic	yellow green	The Balkans	dark pink
Russia	gray	Slovakia	green	Albania	light pink

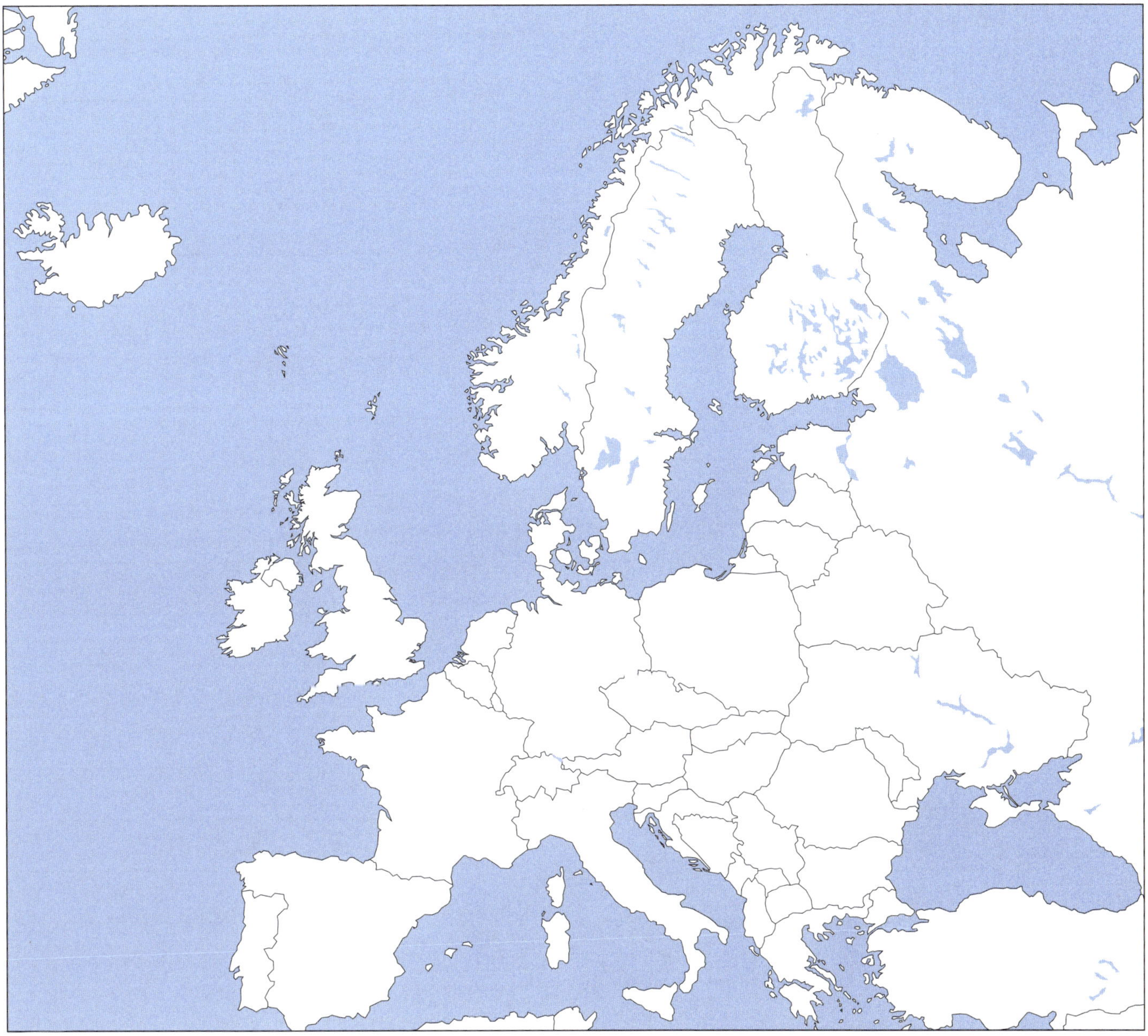

REVIEW

Scandinavia & Eastern Europe

Copy the names of the countries and their capitals below. Pay close attention to correct spelling.

1. Country: Norway Capital: Oslo
2. Country: Sweden Capital: Stockholm
3. Country: Denmark Capital: Copenhagen
4. Country: Iceland Capital: Reykjavik
5. Country: Finland Capital: Helsinki
6. Country: Russia Capital: Moscow
7. Country: Belarus Capital: Minsk
8. Country: Ukraine Capital: Kyiv
9. Country: Poland Capital: Warsaw
10. Country: Czech Republic Capital: Prague
11. Country: Slovakia Capital: Bratislava
12. Country: Hungary Capital: Budapest
13. Country: Romania Capital: Bucharest
14. Country: Bulgaria Capital: Sofia
15. Country: Albania Capital: Tirana
16. Country: Moldova Capital: Chisinau
17. Country: Estonia Capital: Tallinn
18. Country: Latvia Capital: Riga
19. Country: Lithuania Capital: Vilnius
20. Country: Croatia Capital: Zagreb
21. Country: Bosnia & Herzegovina Capital: Sarajevo
22. Country: Montenegro Capital: Podgorica
23. Country: North Macedonia Capital: Skopje
24. Country: Kosovo Capital: Pristina
25. Country: Serbia Capital: Belgrade
26. Country: Slovenia Capital: Ljubljana

REVIEW

Scandinavia & Eastern Europe

Use the map below to practice identifying the countries.

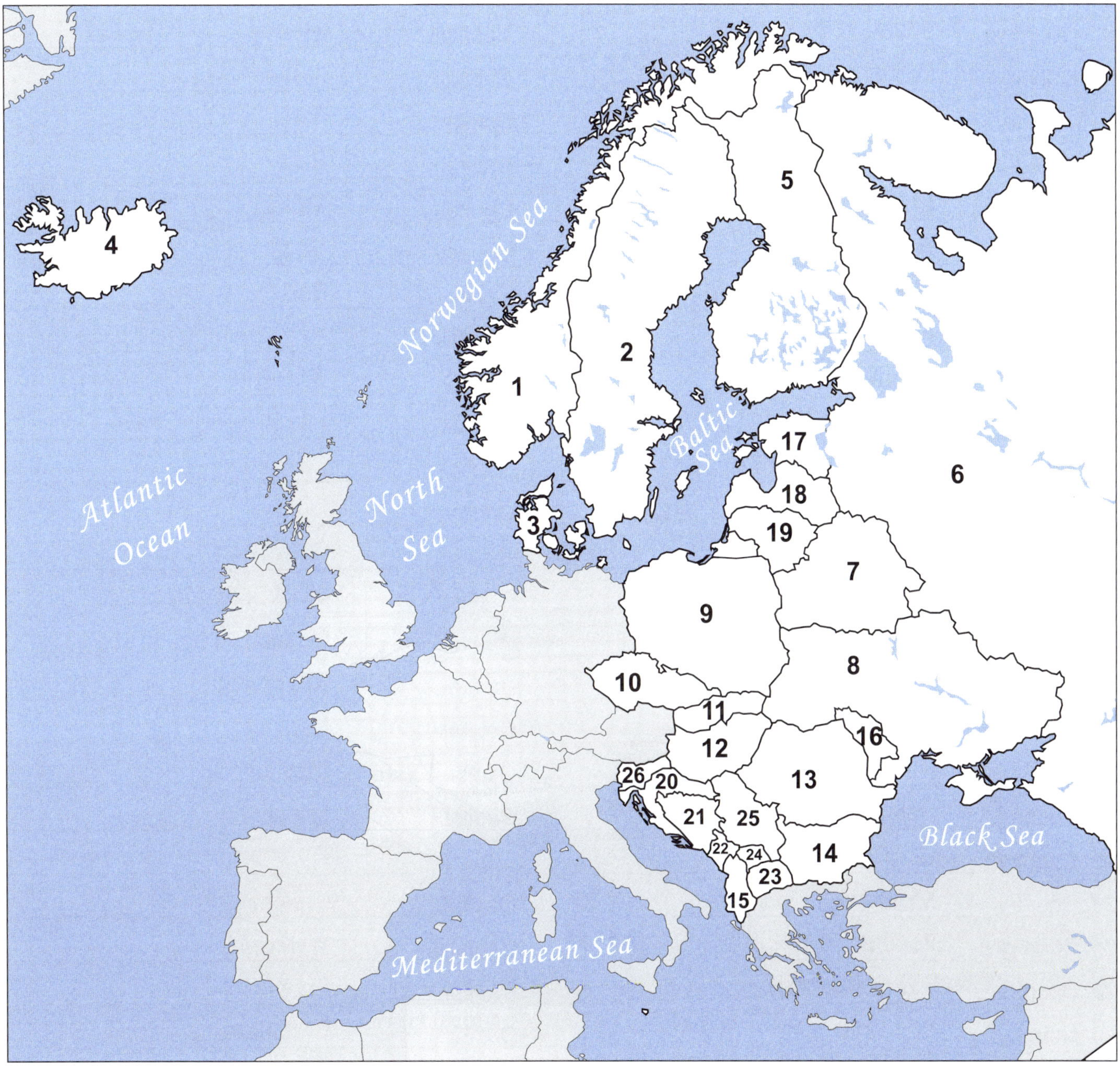

***Note to Teachers*:**
Students should color each of the labeled countries a different color. If time allows, the rest of the countries should be colored the same color, and the bodies of water labeled.

REVIEW

Europe

Copy the names of the countries and their capitals below. Pay close attention to correct spelling.

1. Country: Greece — Capital: Athens
2. Country: Italy — Capital: Rome
3. Country: Spain — Capital: Madrid
4. Country: Portugal — Capital: Lisbon
5. Country: France — Capital: Paris
6. Country: Switzerland — Capital: Bern
7. Country: Liechtenstein — Capital: Vaduz
8. Country: Austria — Capital: Vienna
9. Country: Germany — Capital: Berlin
10. Country: Netherlands — Capital: Amsterdam
11. Country: Belgium — Capital: Brussels
12. Country: Luxembourg — Capital: Luxembourg City
13. Country: United Kingdom — Capital: London
14. Country: Ireland — Capital: Dublin
15. Country: Norway — Capital: Oslo
16. Country: Sweden — Capital: Stockholm
17. Country: Denmark — Capital: Copenhagen
18. Country: Iceland — Capital: Reykjavik
19. Country: Finland — Capital: Helsinki
20. Country: Russia — Capital: Moscow
21. Country: Belarus — Capital: Minsk
22. Country: Ukraine — Capital: Kyiv
23. Country: Moldova — Capital: Chisinau
24. Country: Poland — Capital: Warsaw
25. Country: Czech Republic — Capital: Prague
26. Country: Slovakia — Capital: Bratislava
27. Country: Hungary — Capital: Budapest
28. Country: Romania — Capital: Bucharest
29. Country: Bulgaria — Capital: Sofia
30. Country: Albania — Capital: Tirana
31. Country: Estonia — Capital: Tallinn
32. Country: Latvia — Capital: Riga

REVIEW

Europe

33. Country: Lithuania Capital: Vilnius
34. Country: Croatia Capital: Zagreb
35. Country: Bosnia & Herzegovina Capital: Sarajevo
36. Country: Montenegro Capital: Podgorica
37. Country: North Macedonia Capital: Skopje
38. Country: Kosovo Capital: Pristina
39. Country: Serbia Capital: Belgrade
40. Country: Slovenia Capital: Ljubljana

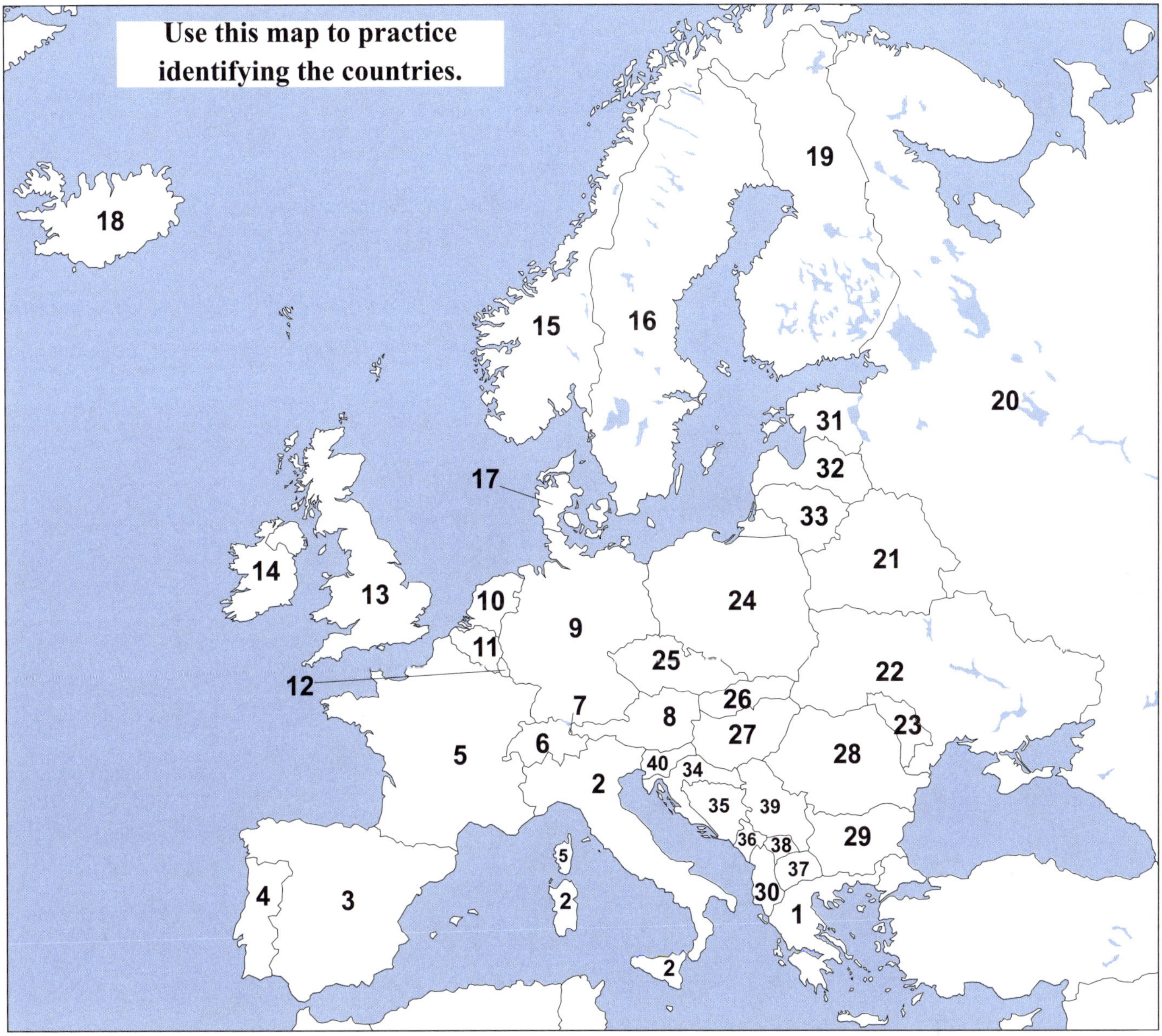

Label and color each of the countries you have studied.

Note to Teachers:
Students should color each of the labeled countries a different color. If time allows, the rest of the countries should be colored the same color, and the bodies of water labeled.

APPENDIX

COUNTRIES & CAPITALS

MIDDLE EAST

Country	Capital
Afghanistan	Kabul
Iran	Tehran
Iraq	Baghdad
Israel	Jerusalem
Jordan	Amman
Lebanon	Beirut
Pakistan	Islamabad
Saudi Arabia	Riyadh
Syria	Damascus
Turkey	Ankara

NORTH AFRICA

Country	Capital
Algeria	Algiers
Egypt	Cairo
Libya	Tripoli
Morocco	Rabat
South Sudan	Juba
Sudan	Khartoum
Tunisia	Tunis

EUROPE

Country	Capital
Albania	Tirana
Austria	Vienna
Belarus	Minsk
Belgium	Brussels
Bosnia & Herzegovina	Sarajevo
Bulgaria	Sofia
Croatia	Zagreb
Czech Republic	Prague
Denmark	Copenhagen
Estonia	Tallinn
Finland	Helsinki
France	Paris
Germany	Berlin
Greece	Athens
Hungary	Budapest
Iceland	Reykjavik
Ireland	Dublin
Italy	Rome
Kosovo	Pristina
Latvia	Riga
Liechtenstein	Vaduz
Lithuania	Vilnius
Luxembourg	Luxembourg City
Moldova	Chisinau
Montenegro	Podgorica
Netherlands	Amsterdam
North Macedonia	Skopje
Norway	Oslo
Poland	Warsaw
Portugal	Lisbon
Romania	Bucharest
Russia	Moscow
Serbia	Belgrade
Slovakia	Bratislava
Slovenia	Ljubljana
Spain	Madrid
Sweden	Stockholm
Switzerland	Bern
United Kingdom	London
Ukraine	Kyiv

REPRODUCIBLE MAPS

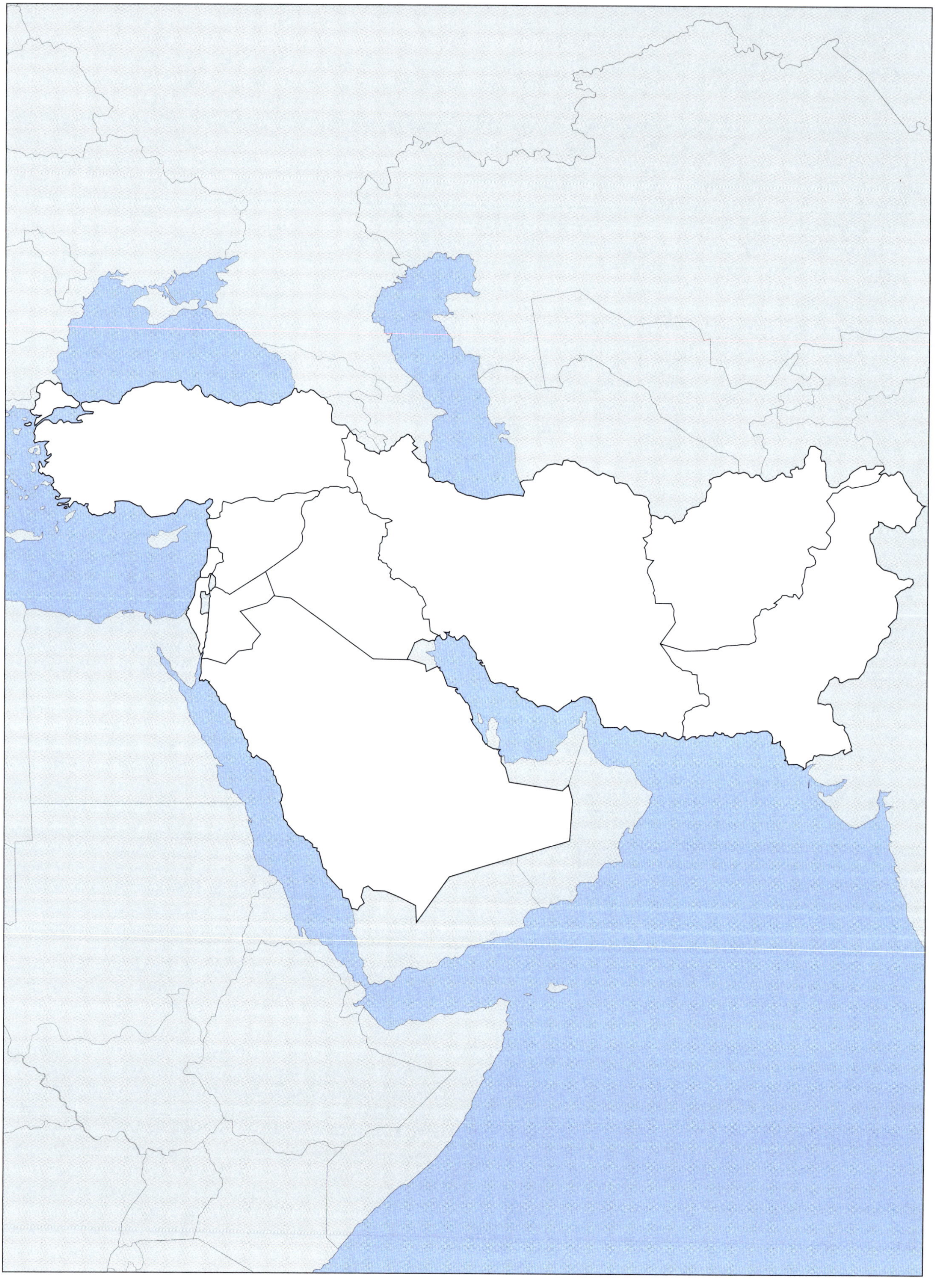

QUIZZES & TESTS

QUIZ 1

The Middle East: Part I

Name:______________________________ Date:______________________

Score:____________

Use the map to fill out the blanks below. Remember to use correct spelling.

1. Country: ______________________ Capital: ______________________
2. Country: ______________________ Capital: ______________________
3. Country: ______________________ Capital: ______________________
4. Country: ______________________ Capital: ______________________

QUIZ 2

The Middle East: Part II

Name:______________________________ Date:____________________

Score:____________

Use the map to fill out the blanks below. Remember to use correct spelling.

1. Country: ____________________ Capital: ____________________
2. Country: ____________________ Capital: ____________________
3. Country: ____________________ Capital: ____________________
4. Country: ____________________ Capital: ____________________
5. Country: ____________________ Capital: ____________________
6. Country: ____________________ Capital: ____________________

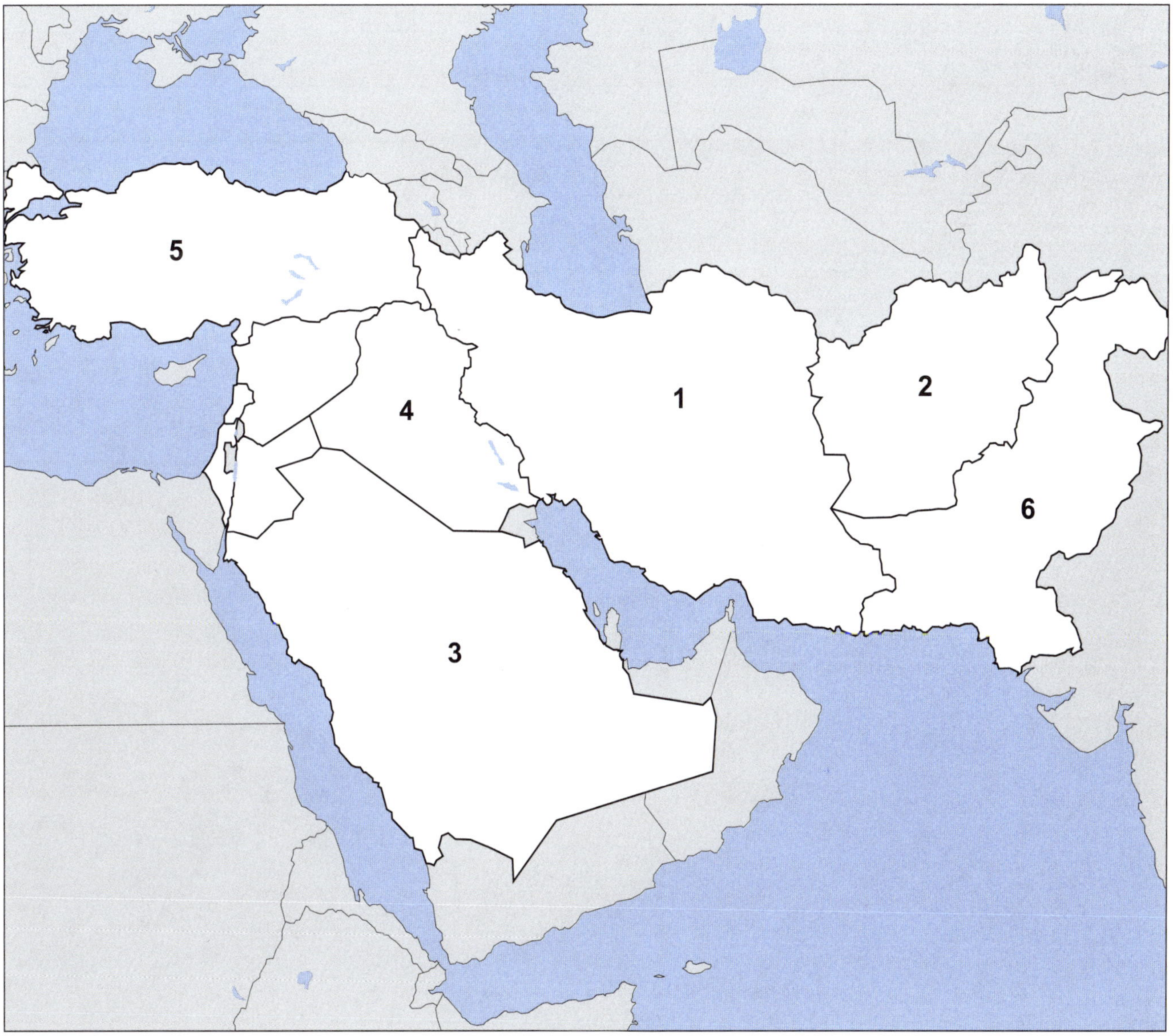

TEST

The Middle East

Name:______________________________ Date:____________________

Score:____________

Use the map to fill out the blanks below. Remember to use correct spelling.

1. Country: ______________________ Capital: ______________________
2. Country: ______________________ Capital: ______________________
3. Country: ______________________ Capital: ______________________
4. Country: ______________________ Capital: ______________________
5. Country: ______________________ Capital: ______________________
6. Country: ______________________ Capital: ______________________
7. Country: ______________________ Capital: ______________________
8. Country: ______________________ Capital: ______________________
9. Country: ______________________ Capital: ______________________
10. Country: ______________________ Capital: ______________________

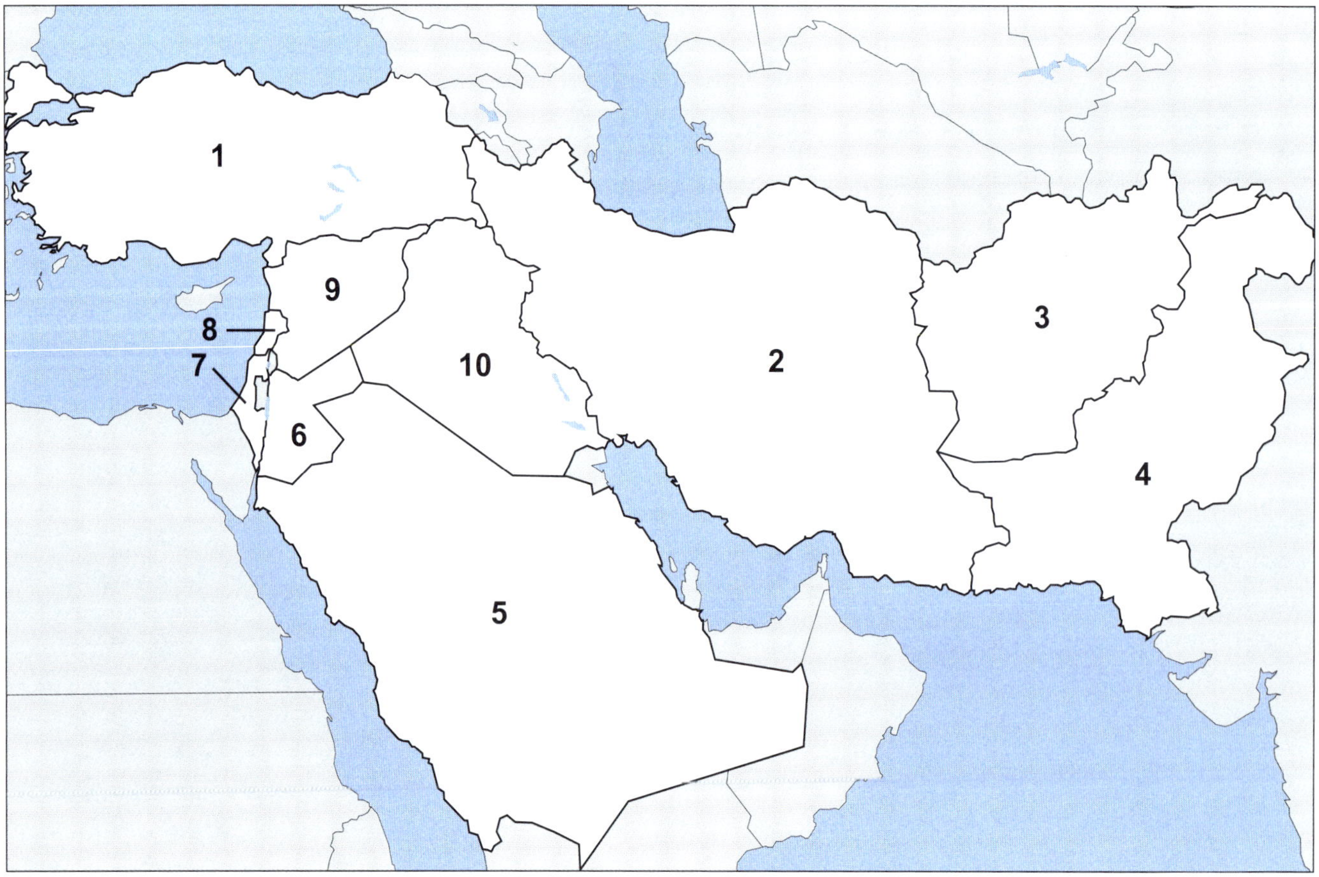

TEST

North Africa

Name:_______________________________________ Date:_______________________

Score:_____________

Use the map to fill out the blanks below. Remember to use correct spelling.

1. Country: ______________________ Capital: ______________________
2. Country: ______________________ Capital: ______________________
3. Country: ______________________ Capital: ______________________
4. Country: ______________________ Capital: ______________________
5. Country: ______________________ Capital: ______________________
6. Country: ______________________ Capital: ______________________
7. Country: ______________________ Capital: ______________________

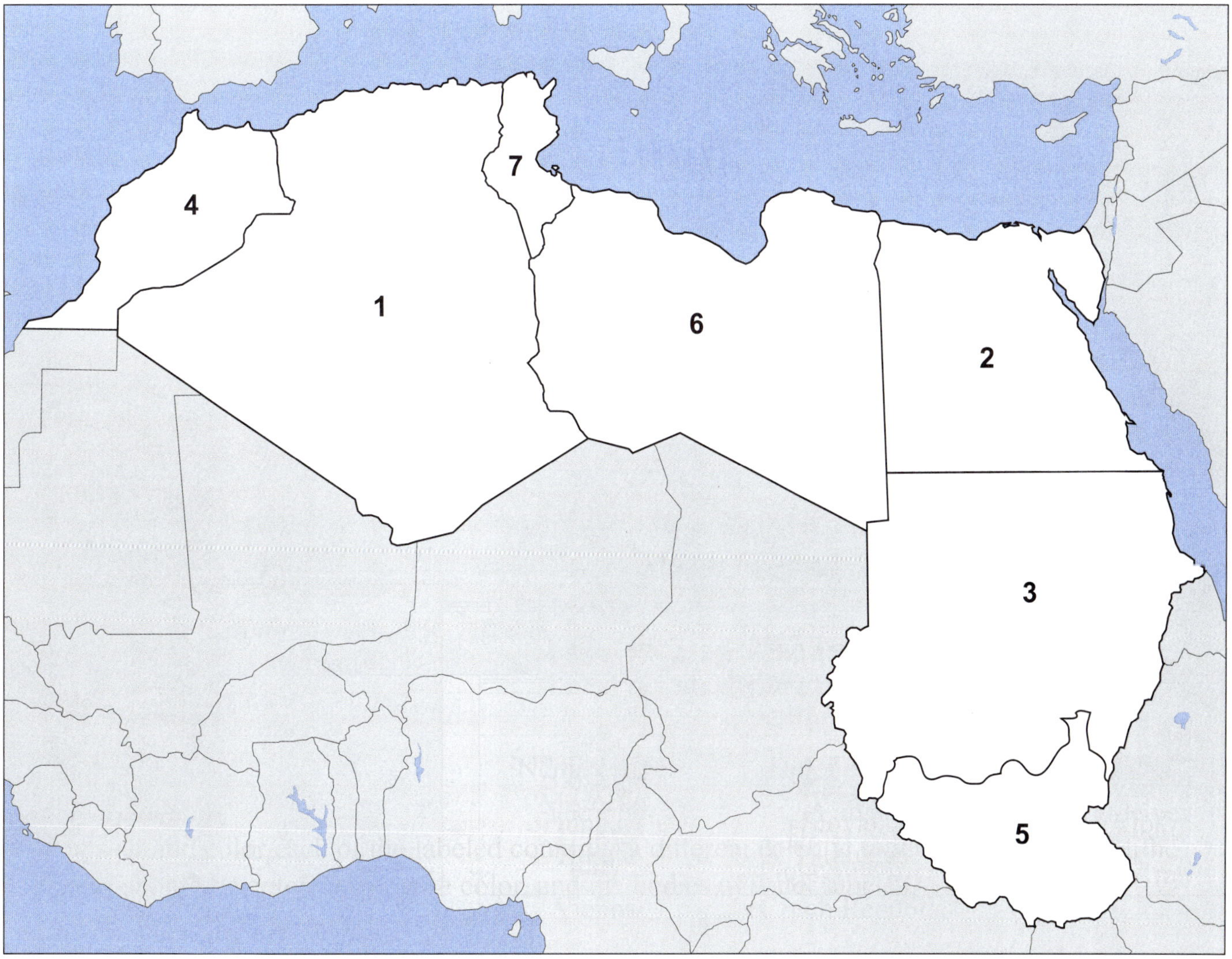

QUIZ 1

Mediterranean Europe

Name:________________________ Date:________________________

Score:______________

Use the map to fill out the blanks below. Remember to use correct spelling.

1. Country: ______________________ Capital: ______________________
2. Country: ______________________ Capital: ______________________
3. Country: ______________________ Capital: ______________________
4. Country: ______________________ Capital: ______________________

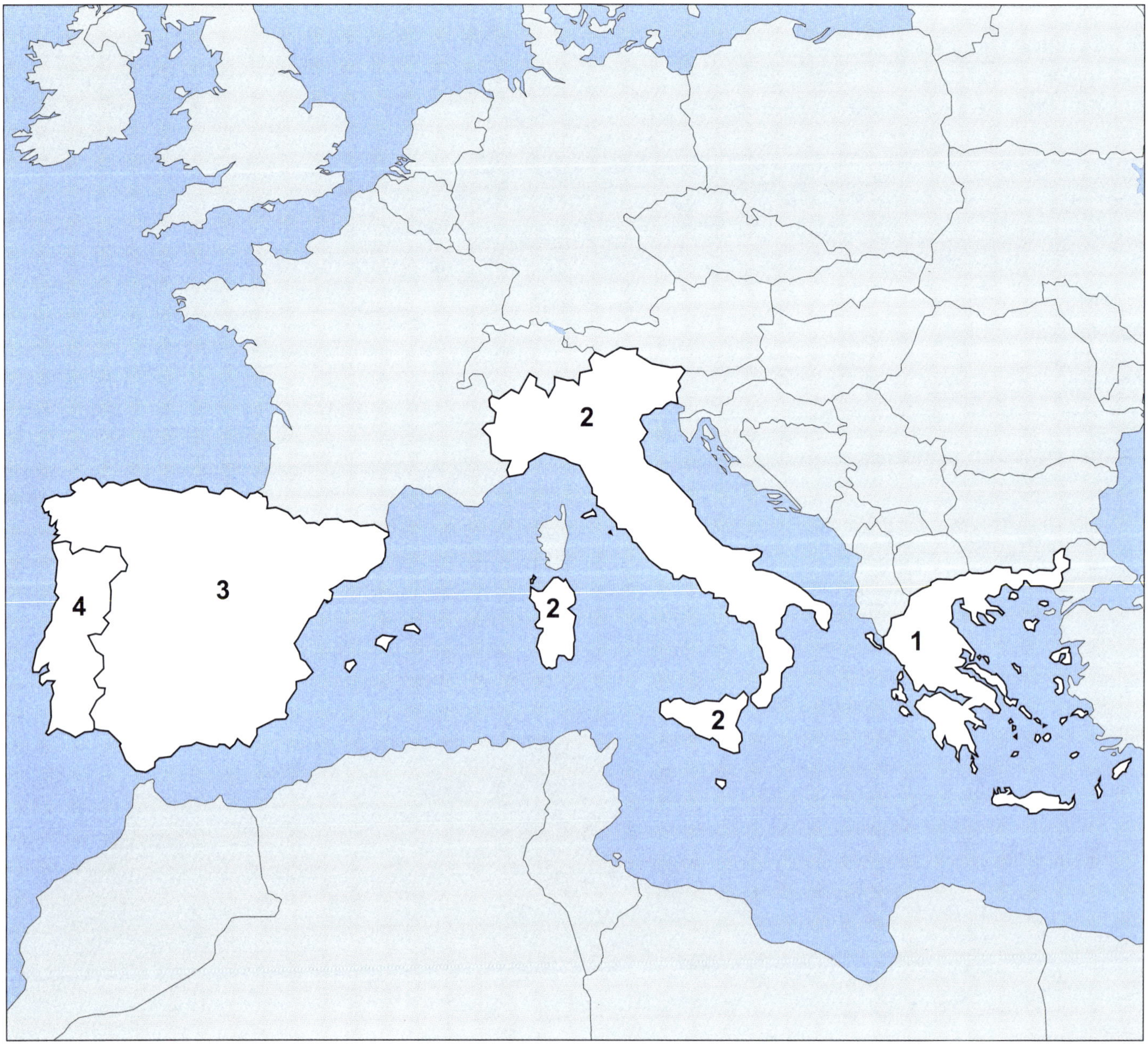

QUIZ 2

Central Europe

Name:______________________________ Date:______________________

Score:______________

Use the map to fill out the blanks below. Remember to use correct spelling.

1. Country: ______________________ Capital: ______________________
2. Country: ______________________ Capital: ______________________
3. Country: ______________________ Capital: ______________________
4. Country: ______________________ Capital: ______________________
5. Country: ______________________ Capital: ______________________

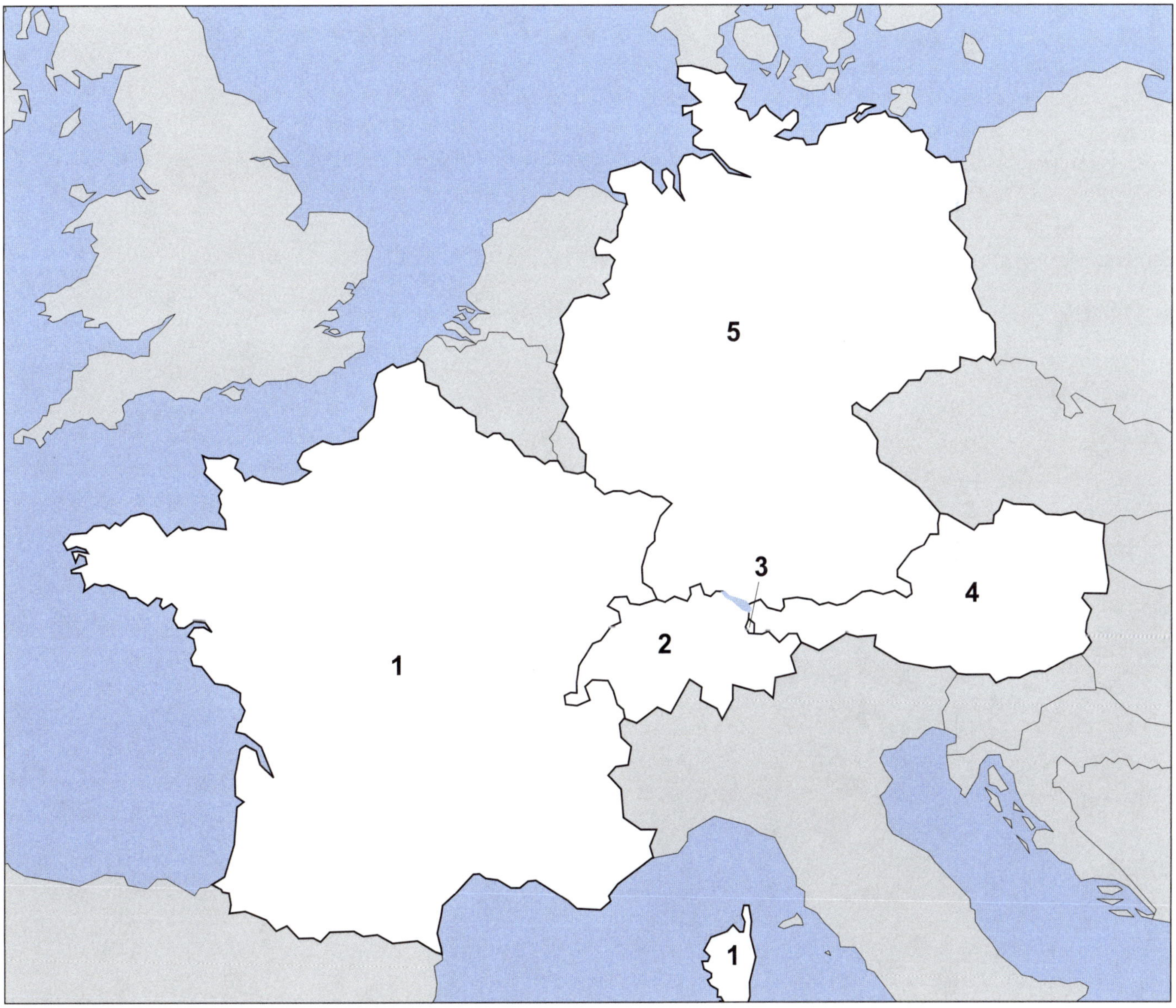

QUIZ 3

The British Isles and the Low Countries

Name:______________________________ Date:____________________

Score:____________

Use the map to fill out the blanks below. Remember to use correct spelling.

1. Country: ______________________ Capital: ______________________
2. Country: ______________________ Capital: ______________________
3. Country: ______________________ Capital: ______________________
4. Country: ______________________ Capital: ______________________
5. Country: ______________________ Capital: ______________________

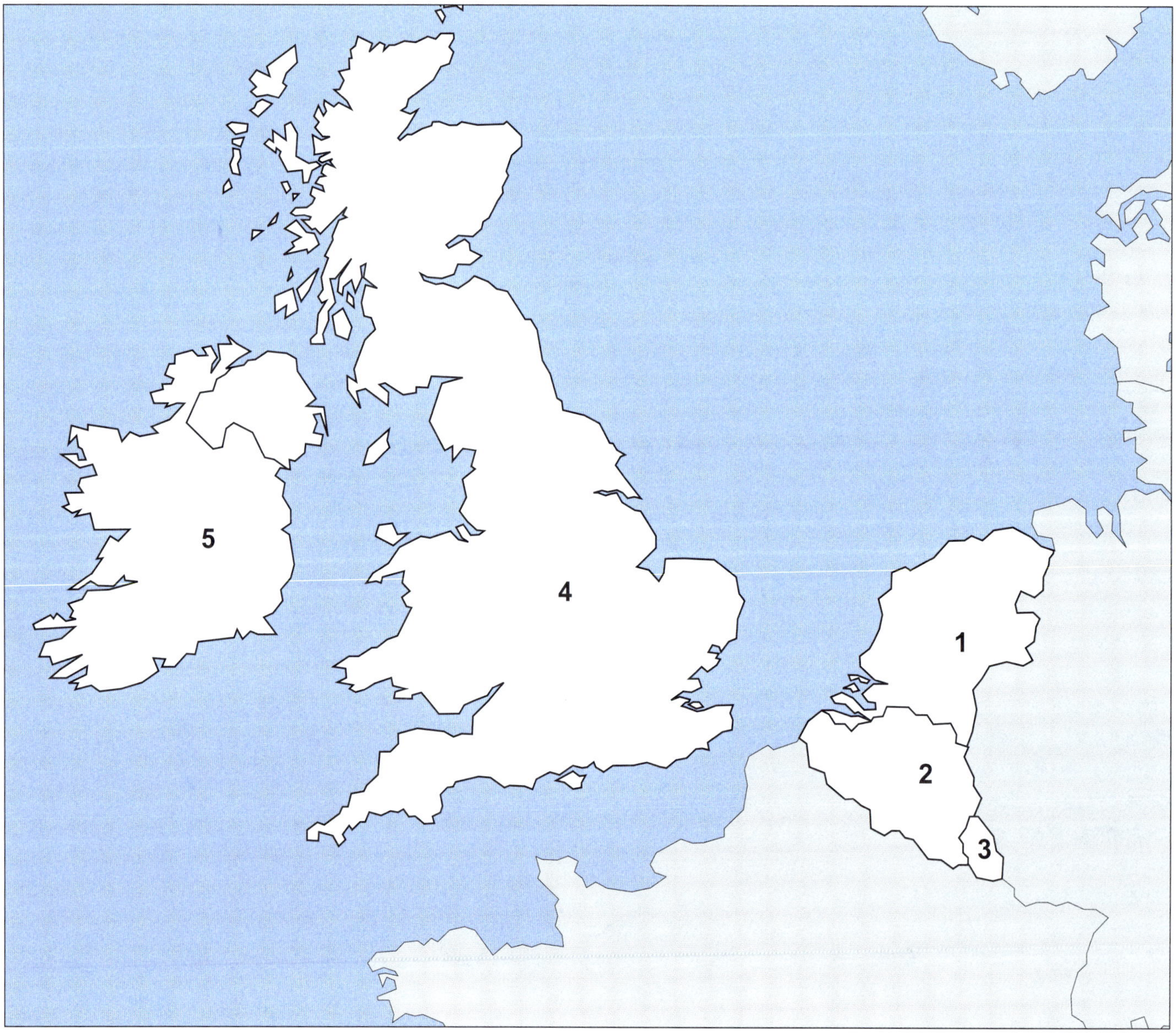

TEST

Europe: Part I

Name:______________________________ Date:____________________

Score:______________

Use the map to fill out the blanks below. Remember to use correct spelling.

1. Country: ______________________ Capital: ______________________
2. Country: ______________________ Capital: ______________________
3. Country: ______________________ Capital: ______________________
4. Country: ______________________ Capital: ______________________
5. Country: ______________________ Capital: ______________________
6. Country: ______________________ Capital: ______________________
7. Country: ______________________ Capital: ______________________
8. Country: ______________________ Capital: ______________________
9. Country: ______________________ Capital: ______________________
10. Country: ______________________ Capital: ______________________
11. Country: ______________________ Capital: ______________________
12. Country: ______________________ Capital: ______________________
13. Country: ______________________ Capital: ______________________
14. Country: ______________________ Capital: ______________________

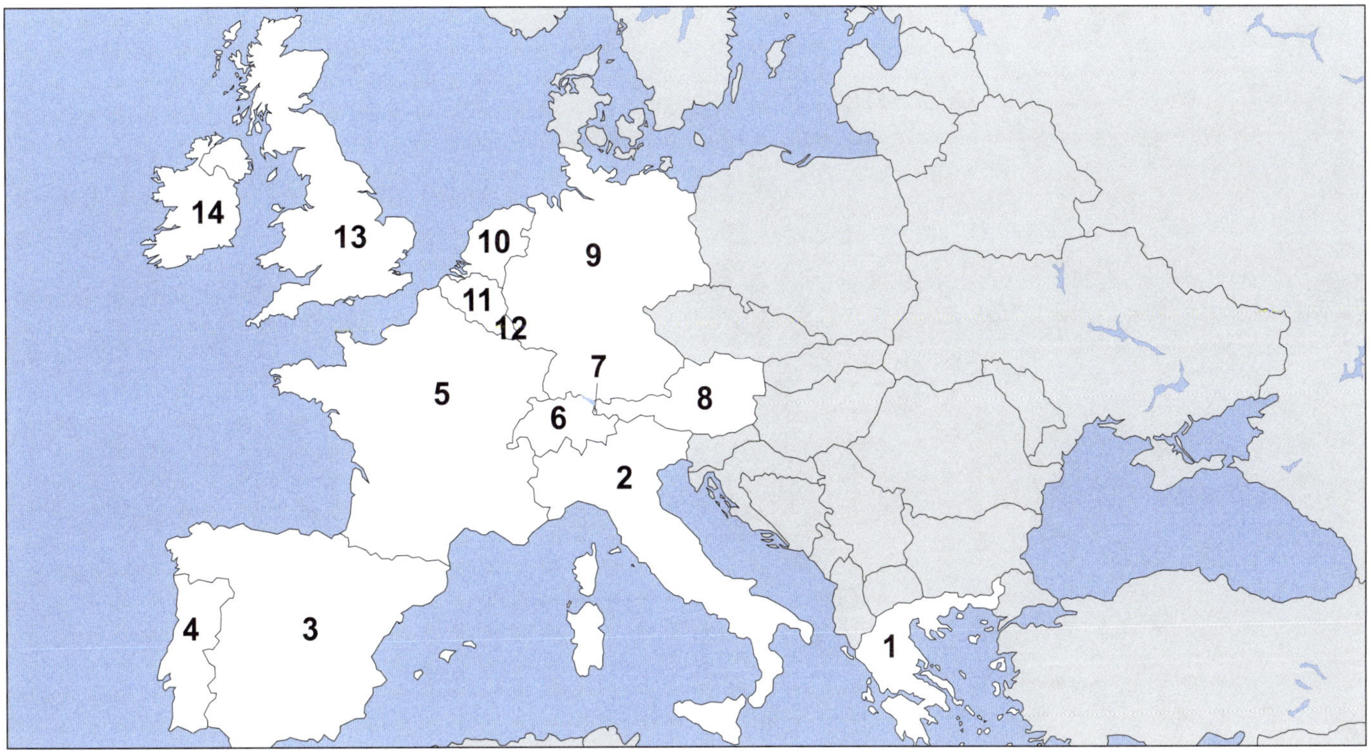

QUIZ 1

Scandinavia

Name:______________________________ Date:____________________

Score:__________

Use the map to fill out the blanks below. Remember to use correct spelling.

1. Country: ____________________ Capital: ____________________
2. Country: ____________________ Capital: ____________________
3. Country: ____________________ Capital: ____________________
4. Country: ____________________ Capital: ____________________
5. Country: ____________________ Capital: ____________________

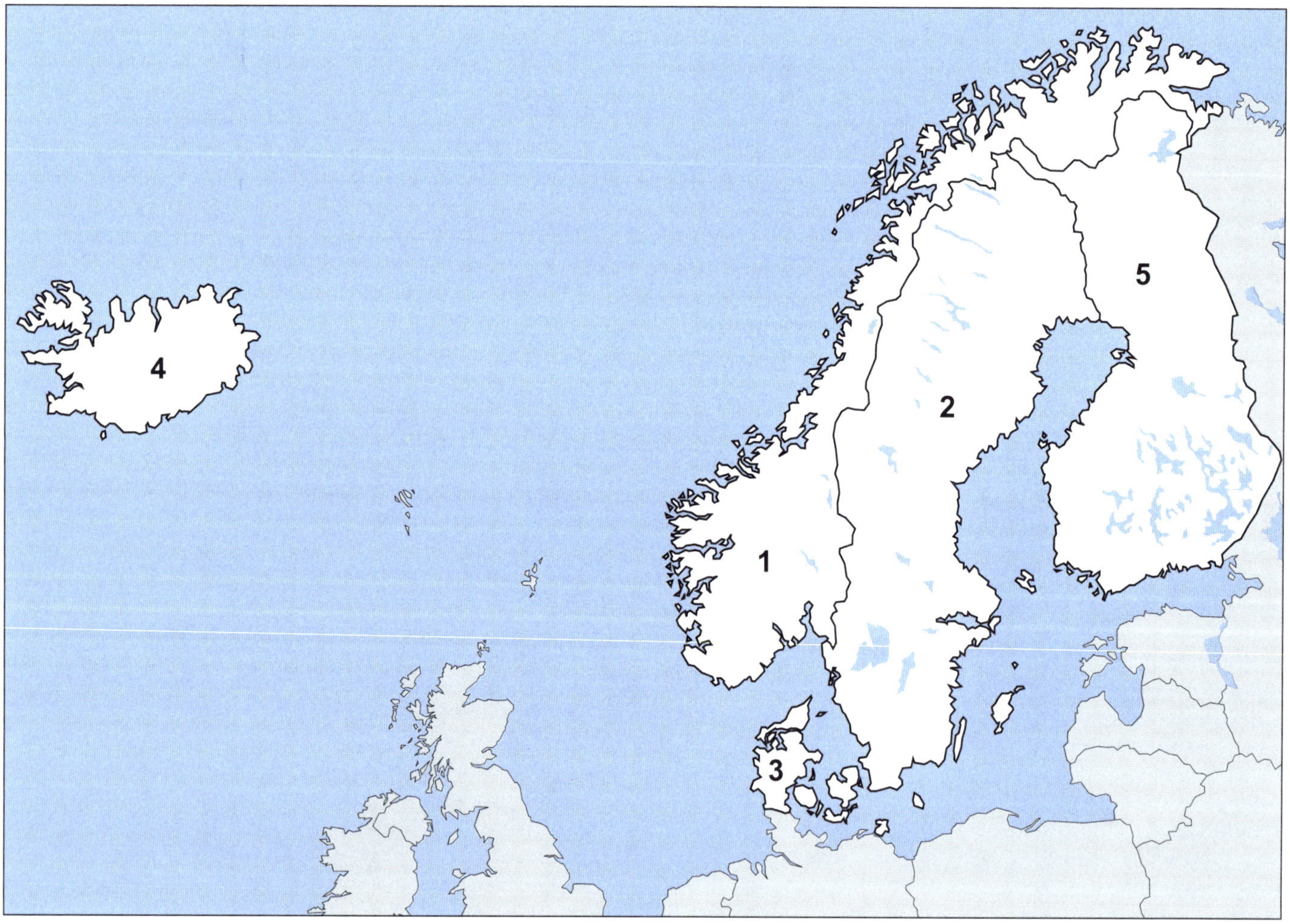

QUIZ 2

Eastern Europe: Part I

Name:_______________________________ Date:_______________________

Score:______________

Use the map to fill out the blanks below. Remember to use correct spelling.

1. Country: ________________________ Capital: ________________________
2. Country: ________________________ Capital: ________________________
3. Country: ________________________ Capital: ________________________
4. Country: ________________________ Capital: ________________________
5. Country: ________________________ Capital: ________________________
6. Country: ________________________ Capital: ________________________
7. Country: ________________________ Capital: ________________________

QUIZ 3

Eastern Europe: Part II

Name:______________________________ Date:____________________

Score:__________

Use the map to fill out the blanks below. Remember to use correct spelling.

1. Country: ____________________ Capital: ____________________
2. Country: ____________________ Capital: ____________________
3. Country: ____________________ Capital: ____________________
4. Country: ____________________ Capital: ____________________
5. Country: ____________________ Capital: ____________________
6. Country: ____________________ Capital: ____________________
7. Country: ____________________ Capital: ____________________
8. Country: ____________________ Capital: ____________________
9. Country: ____________________ Capital: ____________________
10. Country: ____________________ Capital: ____________________
11. Country: ____________________ Capital: ____________________
12. Country: ____________________ Capital: ____________________
13. Country: ____________________ Capital: ____________________
14. Country: ____________________ Capital: ____________________

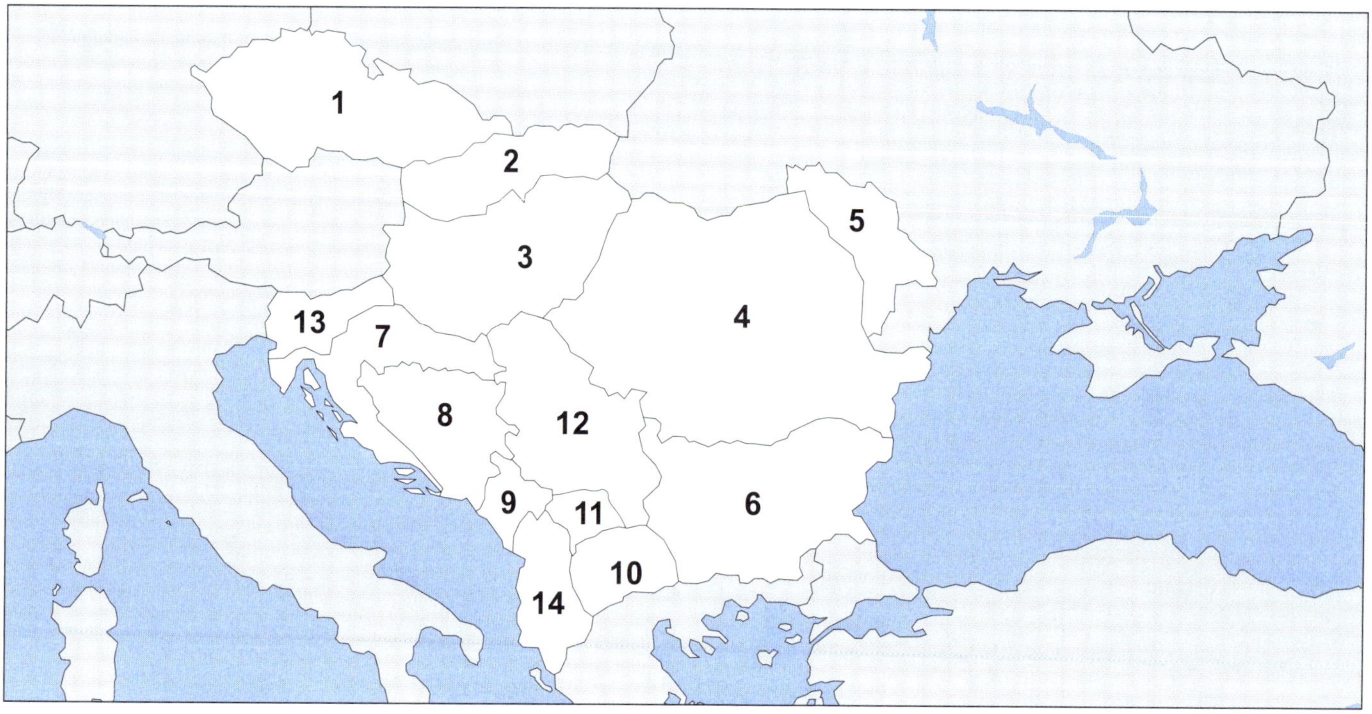

TEST

Europe: Part II

Name:________________________________ Date:____________________

Score:__________

Use the map on the next page to fill out the blanks below. Remember to use correct spelling.

1. Country: ______________________ Capital: ______________________
2. Country: ______________________ Capital: ______________________
3. Country: ______________________ Capital: ______________________
4. Country: ______________________ Capital: ______________________
5. Country: ______________________ Capital: ______________________
6. Country: ______________________ Capital: ______________________
7. Country: ______________________ Capital: ______________________
8. Country: ______________________ Capital: ______________________
9. Country: ______________________ Capital: ______________________
10. Country: ______________________ Capital: ______________________
11. Country: ______________________ Capital: ______________________
12. Country: ______________________ Capital: ______________________
13. Country: ______________________ Capital: ______________________
14. Country: ______________________ Capital: ______________________
15. Country: ______________________ Capital: ______________________
16. Country: ______________________ Capital: ______________________
17. Country: ______________________ Capital: ______________________
18. Country: ______________________ Capital: ______________________
19. Country: ______________________ Capital: ______________________
20. Country: ______________________ Capital: ______________________
21. Country: ______________________ Capital: ______________________
22. Country: ______________________ Capital: ______________________
23. Country: ______________________ Capital: ______________________
24. Country: ______________________ Capital: ______________________
25. Country: ______________________ Capital: ______________________
26. Country: ______________________ Capital: ______________________

TEST

Europe: Part II

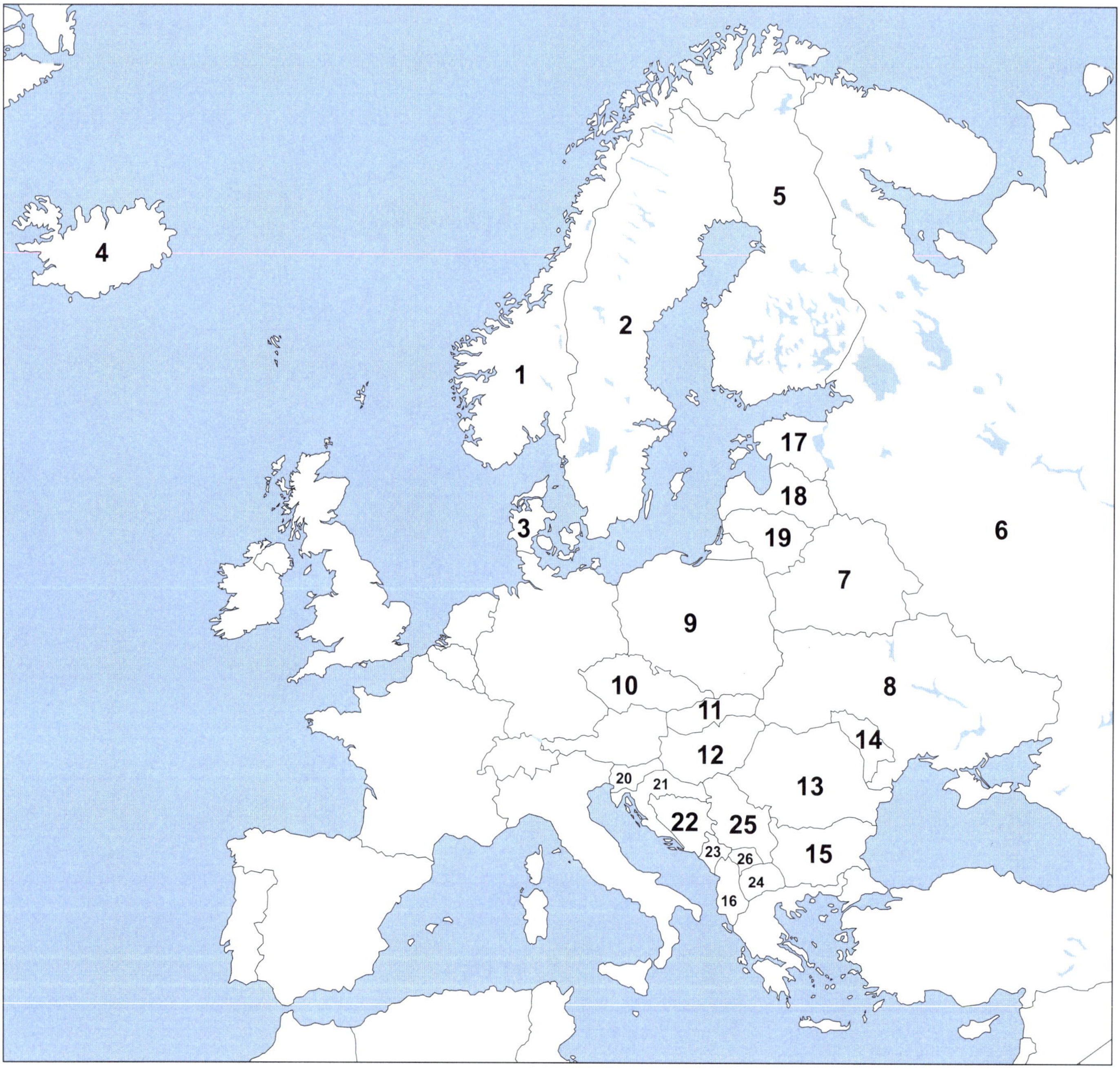

TEST

Europe

Name:______________________________ Date:____________________

Score:__________

Use the map on the next page to fill out the blanks below. Remember to use correct spelling.

1. Country: ______________________ Capital: ______________________
2. Country: ______________________ Capital: ______________________
3. Country: ______________________ Capital: ______________________
4. Country: ______________________ Capital: ______________________
5. Country: ______________________ Capital: ______________________
6. Country: ______________________ Capital: ______________________
7. Country: ______________________ Capital: ______________________
8. Country: ______________________ Capital: ______________________
9. Country: ______________________ Capital: ______________________
10. Country: ______________________ Capital: ______________________
11. Country: ______________________ Capital: ______________________
12. Country: ______________________ Capital: ______________________
13. Country: ______________________ Capital: ______________________
14. Country: ______________________ Capital: ______________________
15. Country: ______________________ Capital: ______________________
16. Country: ______________________ Capital: ______________________
17. Country: ______________________ Capital: ______________________
18. Country: ______________________ Capital: ______________________
19. Country: ______________________ Capital: ______________________
20. Country: ______________________ Capital: ______________________
21. Country: ______________________ Capital: ______________________
22. Country: ______________________ Capital: ______________________
23. Country: ______________________ Capital: ______________________
24. Country: ______________________ Capital: ______________________
25. Country: ______________________ Capital: ______________________

TEST

Europe

26. Country: ______________________ Capital: ______________________
27. Country: ______________________ Capital: ______________________
28. Country: ______________________ Capital: ______________________
29. Country: ______________________ Capital: ______________________
30. Country: ______________________ Capital: ______________________
31. Country: ______________________ Capital: ______________________
32. Country: ______________________ Capital: ______________________
33. Country: ______________________ Capital: ______________________
34. Country: ______________________ Capital: ______________________
35. Country: ______________________ Capital: ______________________
36. Country: ______________________ Capital: ______________________
37. Country: ______________________ Capital: ______________________
38. Country: ______________________ Capital: ______________________
39. Country: ______________________ Capital: ______________________
40. Country: ______________________ Capital: ______________________

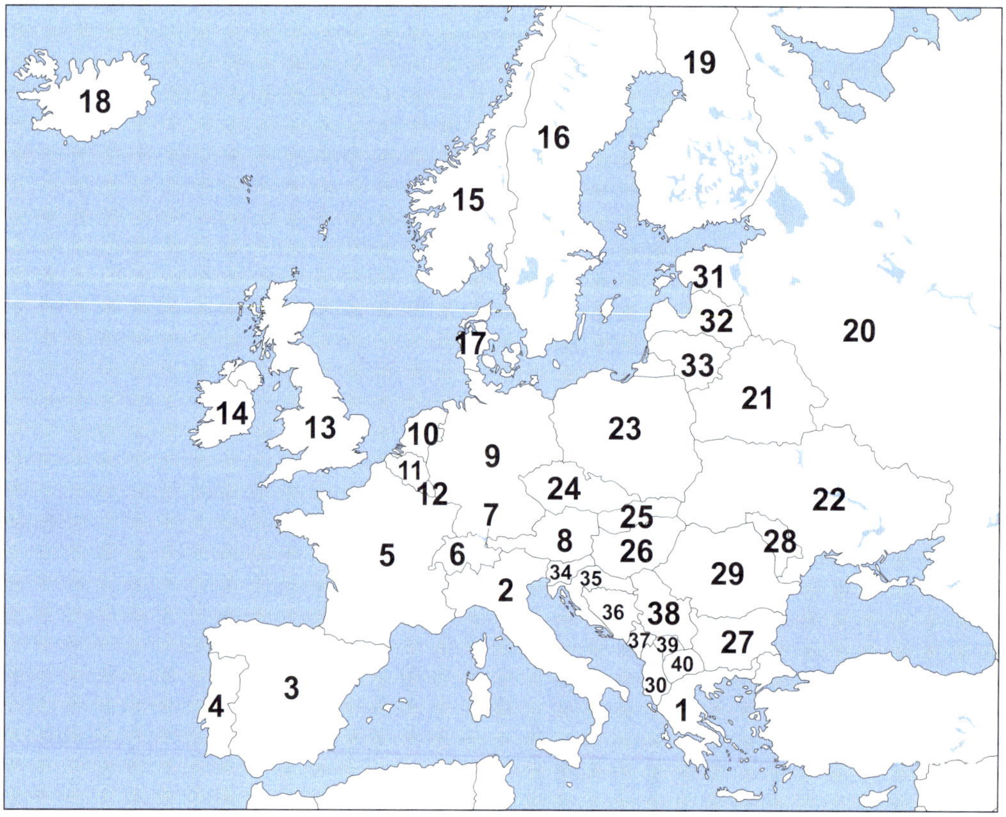

FINAL TEST

Name:____ Date:___________________________

Score:_______________

Use the map to place each country's number next to the name of the country and its capital.

_______ Afghanistan	_______ Ankara
_______ Iran	_______ Tehran
_______ Iraq	_______ Kabul
_______ Israel	_______ Islamabad
_______ Jordan	_______ Riyadh
_______ Lebanon	_______ Amman
_______ Pakistan	_______ Jerusalem
_______ Saudi Arabia	_______ Beirut
_______ Syria	_______ Damascus
_______ Turkey	_______ Baghdad

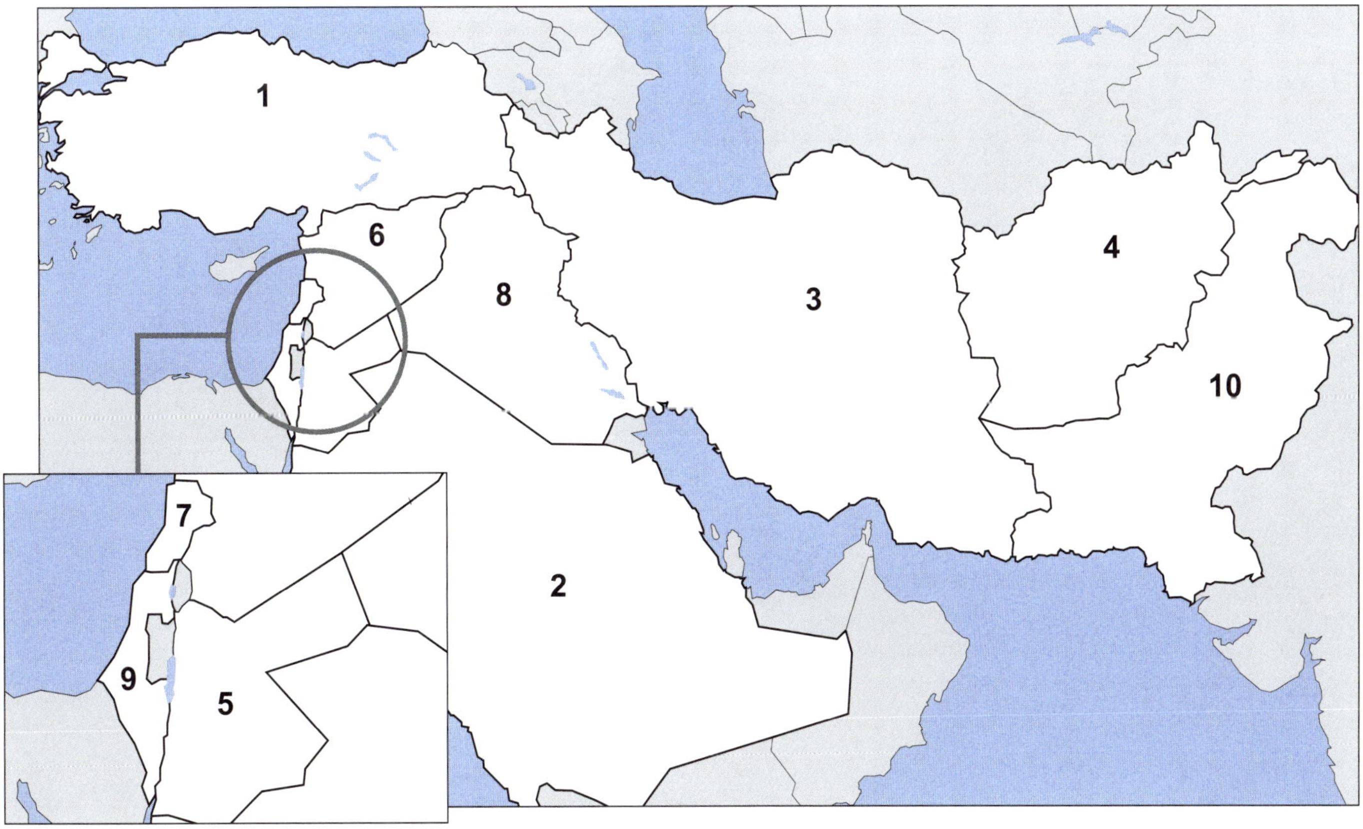

FINAL TEST

Use the map to place each country's number next to the name of the country and its capital.

_______ Algeria

_______ Egypt

_______ Libya

_______ Morocco

_______ Sudan

_______ Tunisia

_______ South Sudan

_______ Rabat

_______ Algiers

_______ Tunis

_______ Juba

_______ Tripoli

_______ Cairo

_______ Khartoum

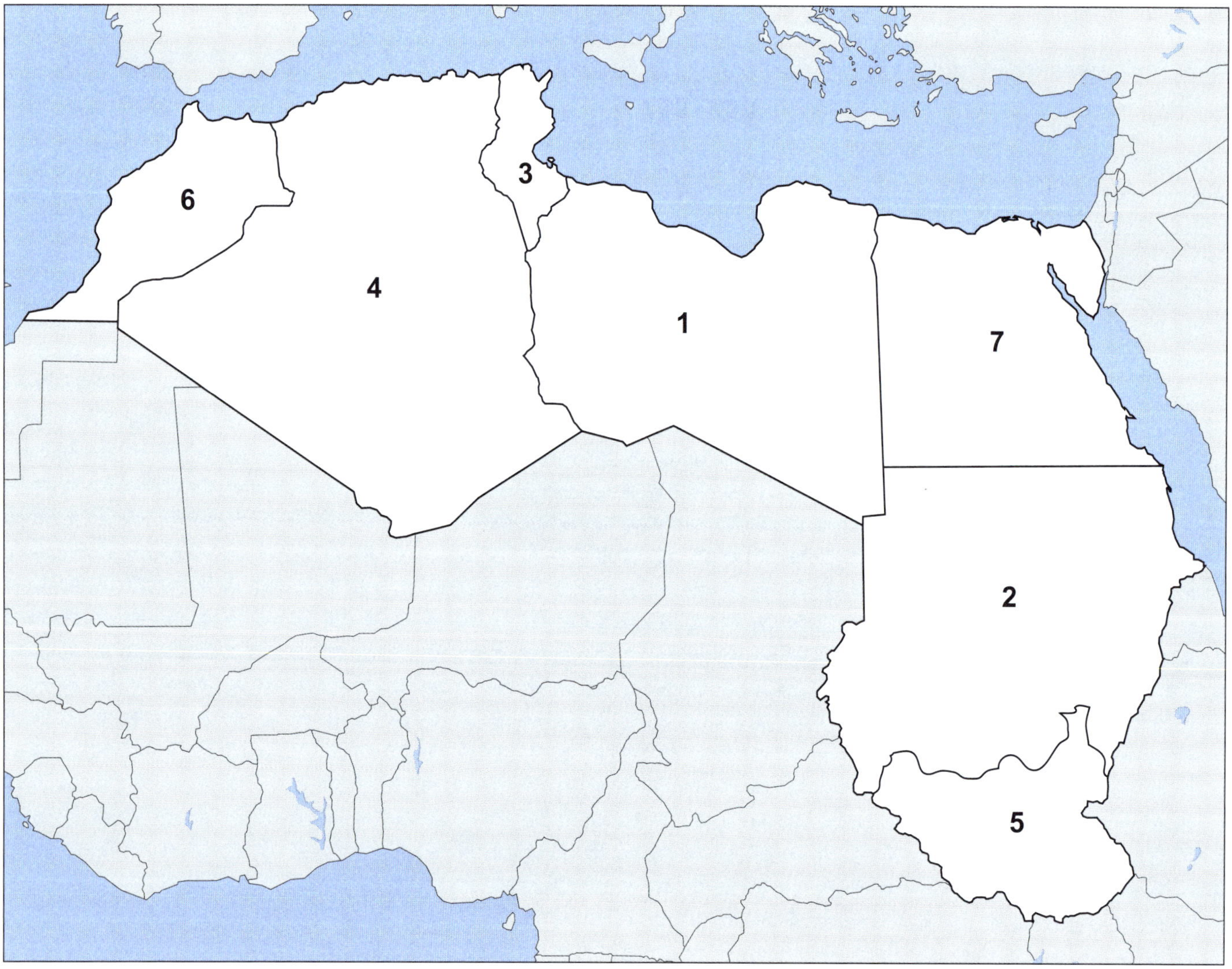

FINAL TEST

Use the map to place each country's number next to the name of the country and its capital.

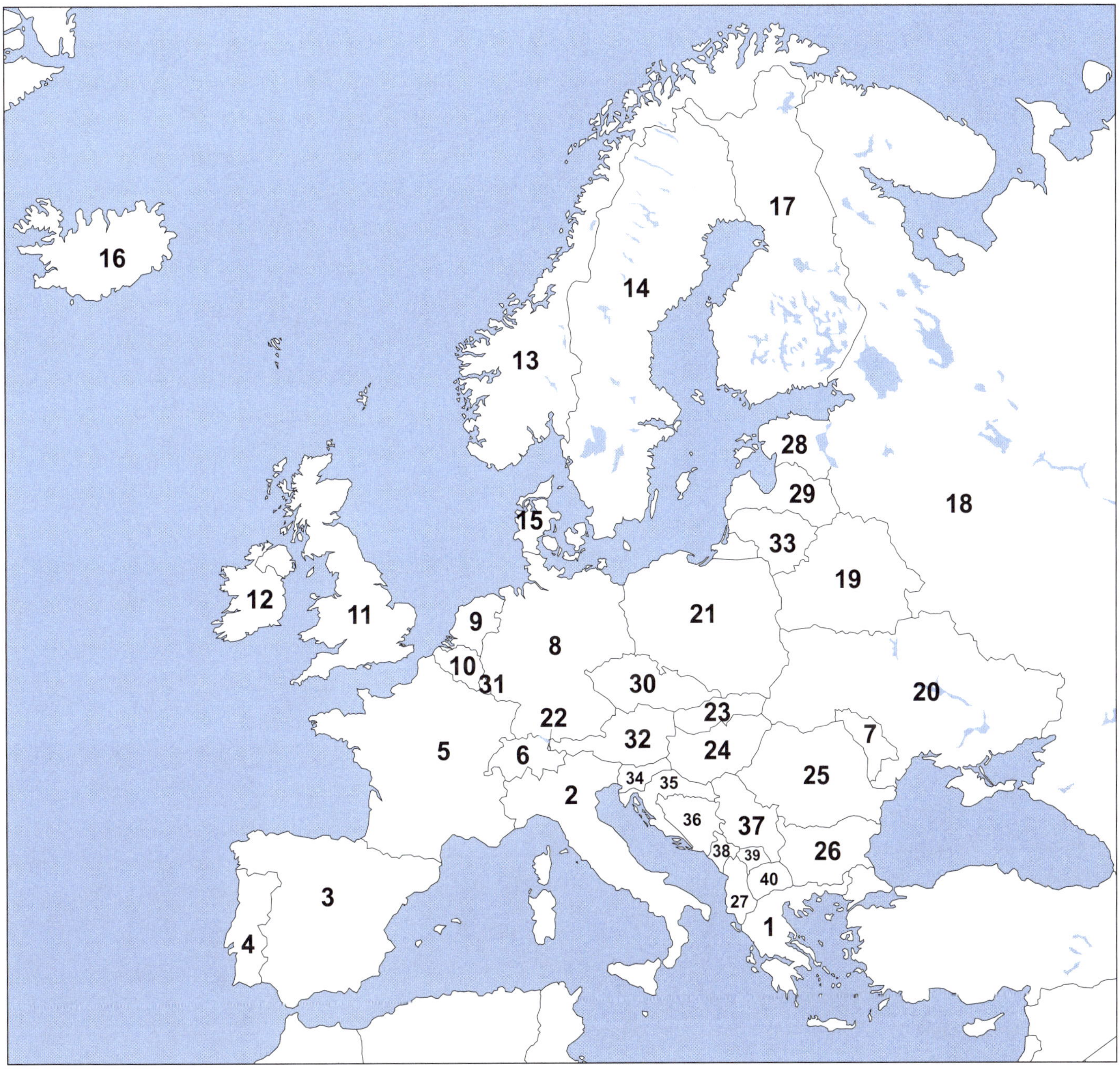

FINAL TEST

COUNTRY

_______ Albania
_______ Austria
_______ Belarus
_______ Belgium
_______ Bulgaria
_______ Bosnia & Herzegovina
_______ Croatia
_______ Czech Republic
_______ Denmark
_______ Estonia
_______ Finland
_______ France
_______ Germany
_______ Greece
_______ Hungary
_______ Iceland
_______ Ireland
_______ Italy
_______ Kosovo
_______ Latvia
_______ Liechtenstein
_______ Lithuania
_______ Luxembourg
_______ North Macedonia
_______ Moldova
_______ Montenegro
_______ Netherlands
_______ Norway
_______ Poland
_______ Portugal
_______ Romania
_______ Russia
_______ Serbia
_______ Slovakia
_______ Slovenia
_______ Spain
_______ Sweden
_______ Switzerland
_______ United Kingdom
_______ Ukraine

CAPITAL

_______ Amsterdam
_______ Athens
_______ Belgrade
_______ Berlin
_______ Bern
_______ Bratislava
_______ Brussels
_______ Bucharest
_______ Budapest
_______ Chisinau
_______ Copenhagen
_______ Dublin
_______ Helsinki
_______ Kyiv
_______ Lisbon
_______ Ljubljana
_______ London
_______ Luxembourg City
_______ Madrid
_______ Minsk
_______ Moscow
_______ Oslo
_______ Paris
_______ Podgorica
_______ Prague
_______ Pristina
_______ Reykjavik
_______ Riga
_______ Rome
_______ Sarajevo
_______ Skopje
_______ Sofia
_______ Stockholm
_______ Tallinn
_______ Tirana
_______ Vaduz
_______ Vienna
_______ Vilnius
_______ Warsaw
_______ Zagreb

QUIZ 1

The Middle East: Part I

ANSWER KEY

Name:________________________________ Date:____________________

Score:______________

Use the map to fill out the blanks below. Remember to use correct spelling.

1. Country: Jordan Capital: Amman
2. Country: Israel Capital: Jerusalem
3. Country: Lebanon Capital: Beirut
4. Country: Syria Capital: Damascus

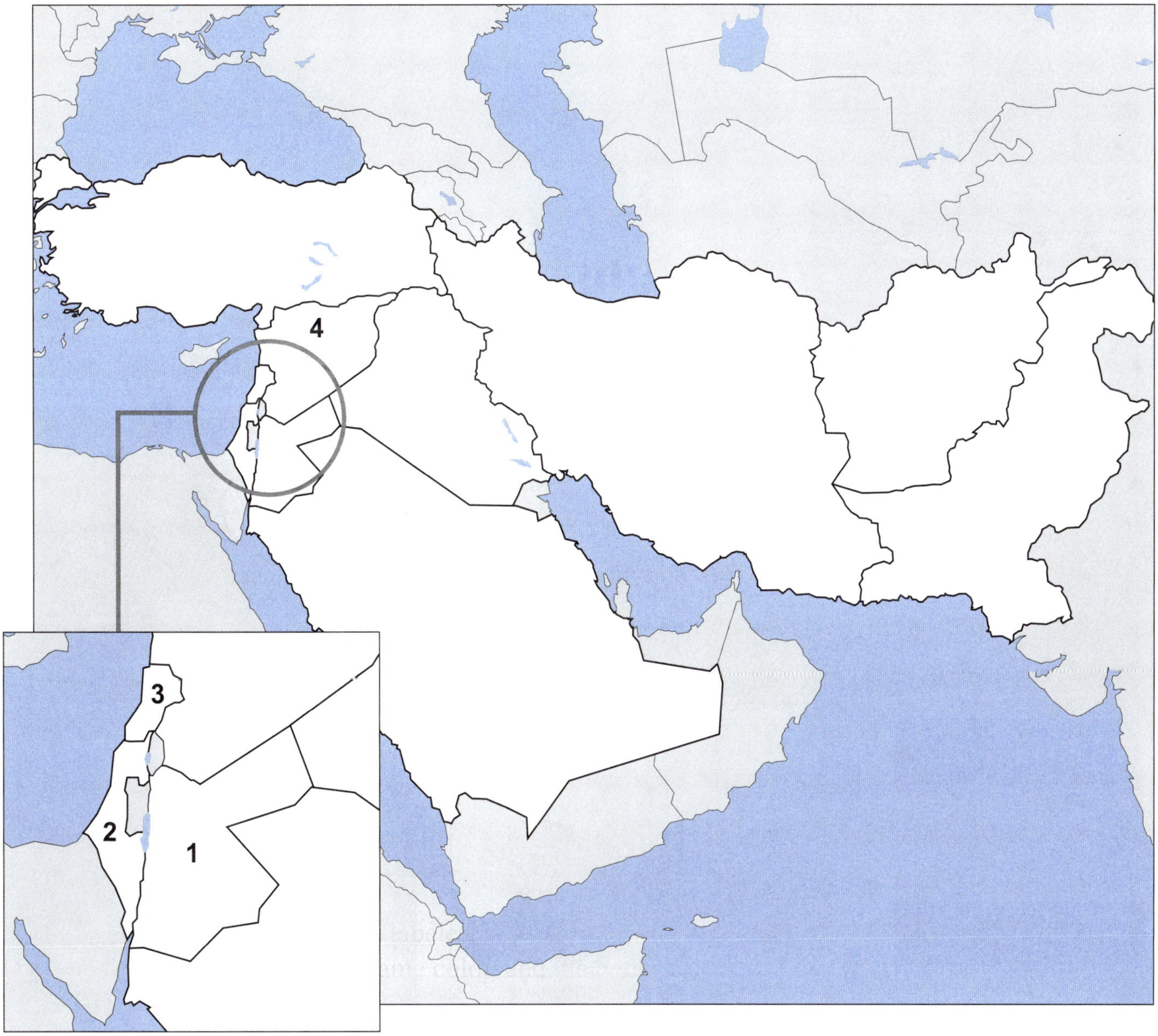

QUIZ 2

ANSWER KEY

The Middle East: Part II

Name:____ Date:__________________________

Score:_______________

Use the map to fill out the blanks below. Remember to use correct spelling.

1. Country: Iran Capital: Tehran
2. Country: Afghanistan Capital: Kabul
3. Country: Saudi Arabia Capital: Riyadh
4. Country: Iraq Capital: Baghdad
5. Country: Turkey Capital: Ankara
6. Country: Pakistan Capital: Islamabad

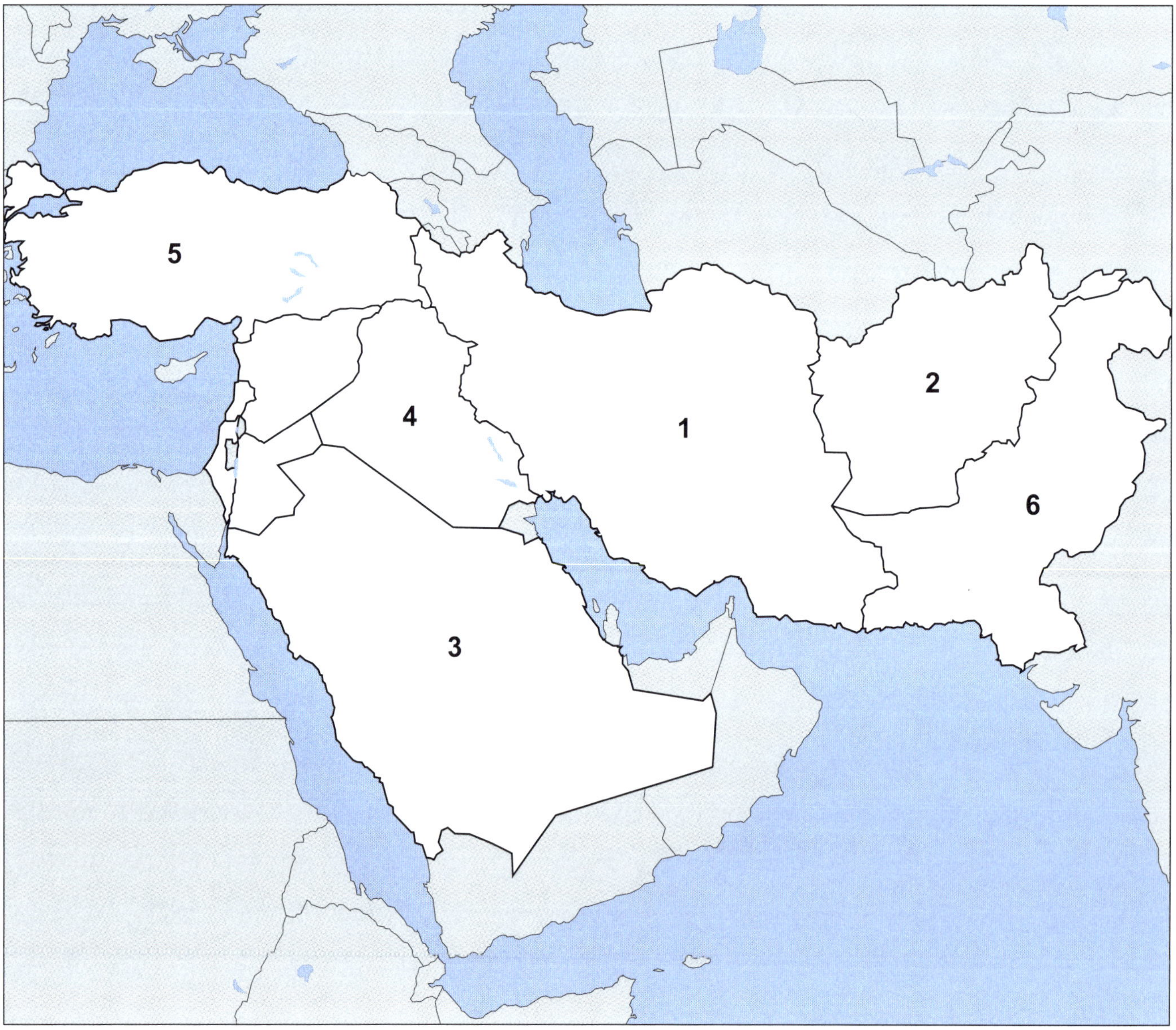

TEST

The Middle East

ANSWER KEY

Name:______________________________ Date:____________________

Score:______________

Use the map to fill out the blanks below. Remember to use correct spelling.

1. Country: Turkey Capital: Ankara
2. Country: Iran Capital: Tehran
3. Country: Afghanistan Capital: Kabul
4. Country: Pakistan Capital: Islamabad
5. Country: Saudi Arabia Capital: Riyadh
6. Country: Jordan Capital: Amman
7. Country: Israel Capital: Jerusalem
8. Country: Lebanon Capital: Beirut
9. Country: Syria Capital: Damascus
10. Country: Iraq Capital: Baghdad

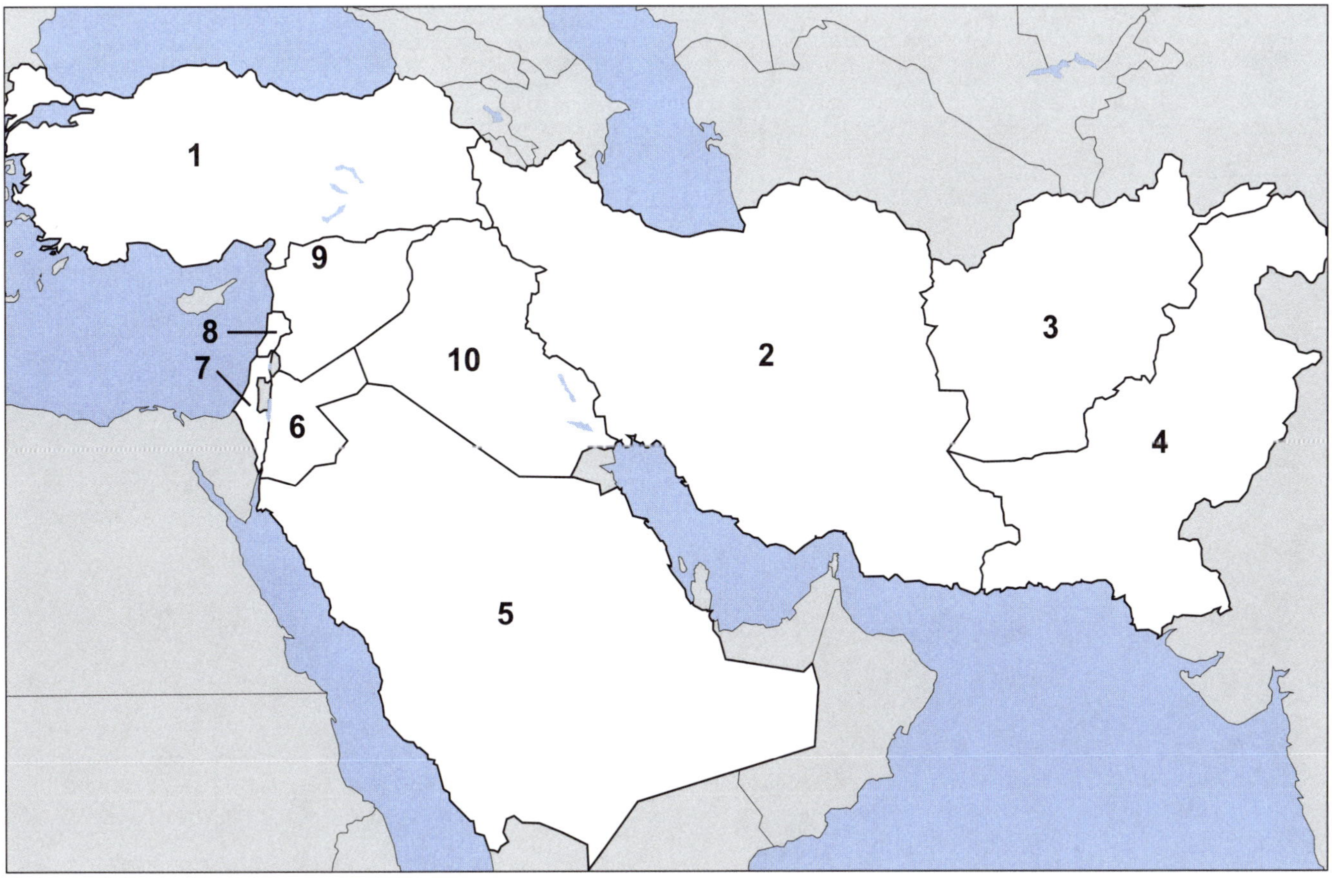

TEST

North Africa

ANSWER KEY

Name:________________________________ Date:____________________

Score:____________

Use the map to fill out the blanks below. Remember to use correct spelling.

1. Country: Algeria Capital: Algiers
2. Country: Egypt Capital: Cairo
3. Country: Sudan Capital: Khartoum
4. Country: Morocco Capital: Rabat
5. Country: South Sudan Capital: Juba
6. Country: Libya Capital: Tripoli
7. Country: Tunisia Capital: Tunis

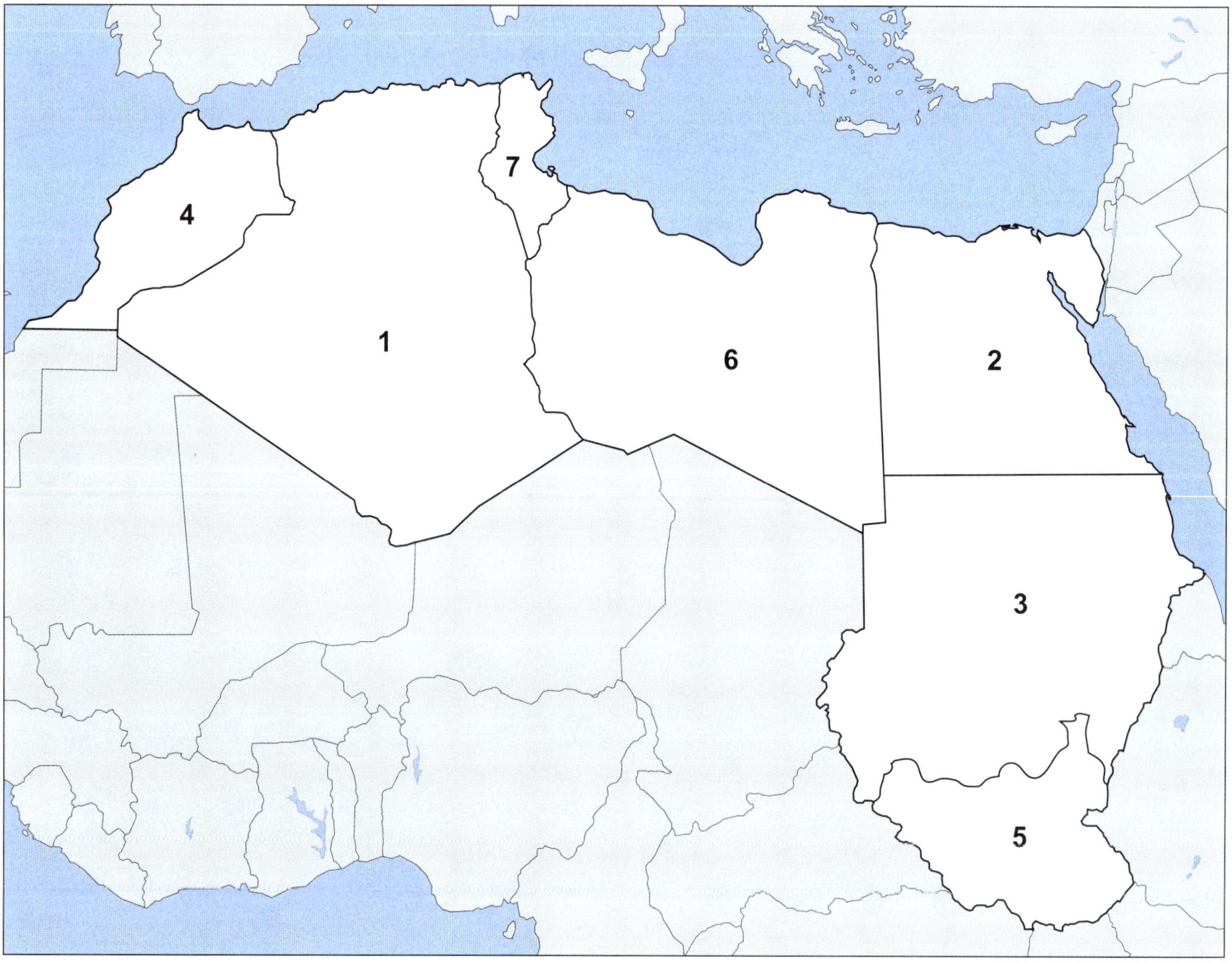

QUIZ 1

Mediterranean Europe

ANSWER KEY

Name:______________________________ Date:____________________

Score:____________

Use the map to fill out the blanks below. Remember to use correct spelling.

1. Country: Greece Capital: Athens
2. Country: Italy Capital: Rome
3. Country: Spain Capital: Madrid
4. Country: Portugal Capital: Lisbon

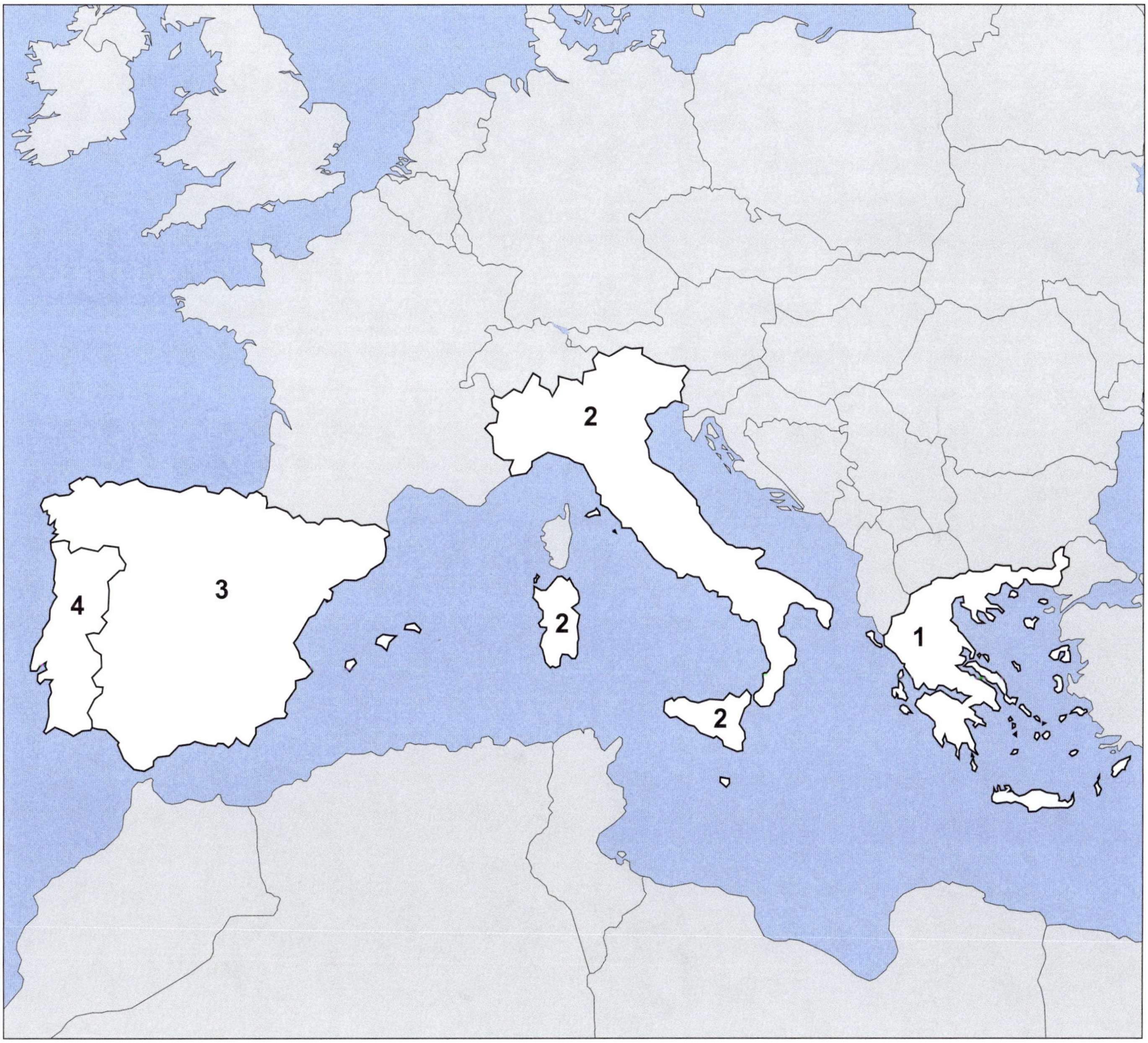

QUIZ 2

Central Europe

ANSWER KEY

Name:______________________________ Date:______________________

Score:______________

Use the map to fill out the blanks below. Remember to use correct spelling.

1. Country: France Capital: Paris
2. Country: Switzerland Capital: Bern
3. Country: Liechtenstein Capital: Vaduz
4. Country: Austria Capital: Vienna
5. Country: Germany Capital: Berlin

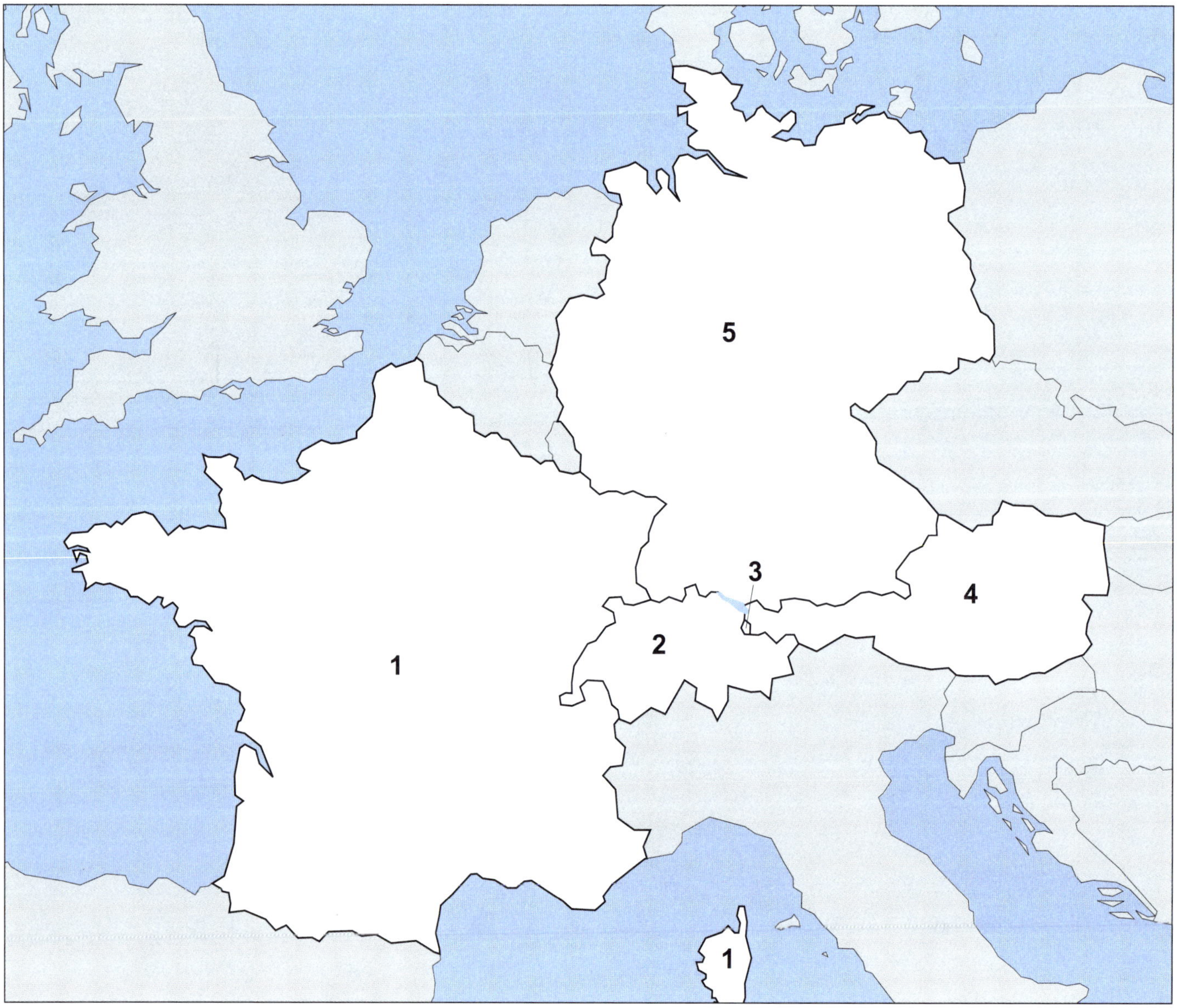

QUIZ 3

The British Isles and the Low Countries

ANSWER KEY

Name:______________________________ Date:______________________

Score:______________

Use the map to fill out the blanks below. Remember to use correct spelling.

1. Country: Netherlands Capital: Amsterdam
2. Country: Belgium Capital: Brussels
3. Country: Luxembourg Capital: Luxembourg City
4. Country: United Kingdom Capital: London
5. Country: Ireland Capital: Dublin

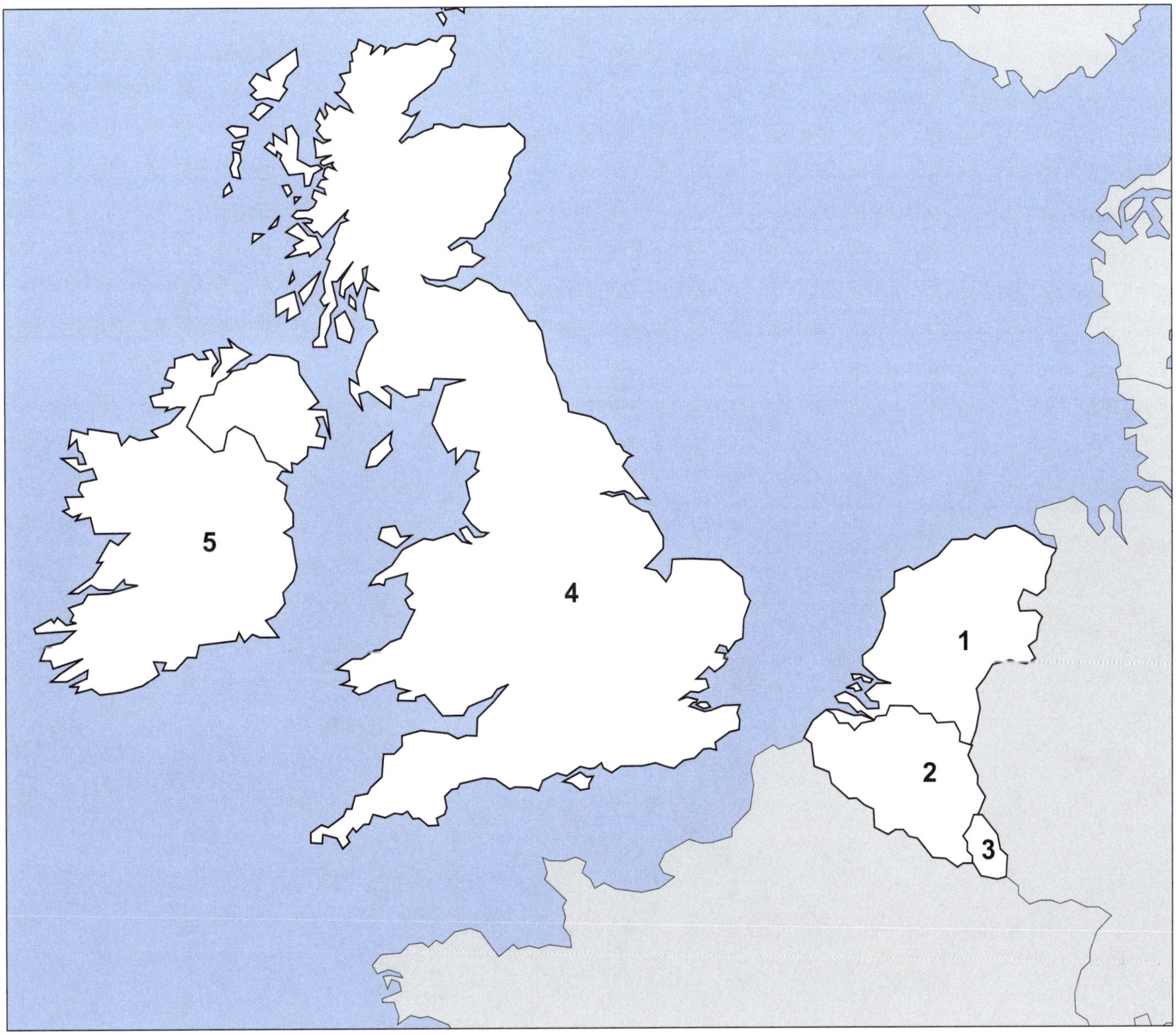

TEST

Europe: Part I

ANSWER KEY

Name:______________________ Date:______________________

Score:______________

Use the map to fill out the blanks below. Remember to use correct spelling.

1. Country: Greece Capital: Athens
2. Country: Italy Capital: Rome
3. Country: Spain Capital: Madrid
4. Country: Portugal Capital: Lisbon
5. Country: France Capital: Paris
6. Country: Switzerland Capital: Bern
7. Country: Liechtenstein Capital: Vaduz
8. Country: Austria Capital: Vienna
9. Country: Germany Capital: Berlin
10. Country: Netherlands Capital: Amsterdam
11. Country: Belgium Capital: Brussels
12. Country: Luxembourg Capital: Luxembourg City
13. Country: United Kingdom Capital: London
14. Country: Ireland Capital: Dublin

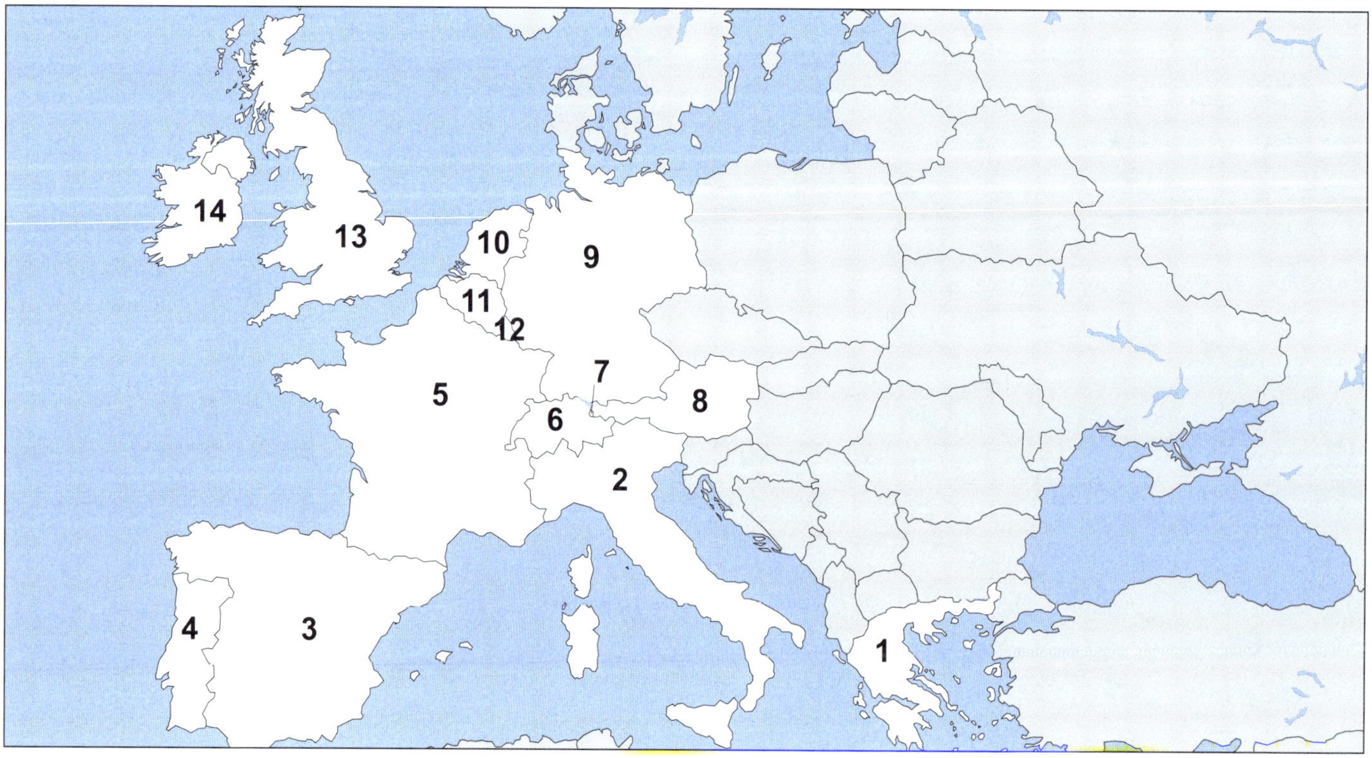

QUIZ 1

Scandinavia

ANSWER KEY

Name:______________________ Date:______________________

Score:______________

Use the map to fill out the blanks below. Remember to use correct spelling.

1. Country: Norway Capital: Oslo
2. Country: Sweden Capital: Stockholm
3. Country: Denmark Capital: Copenhagen
4. Country: Iceland Capital: Reykjavik
5. Country: Finland Capital: Helsinki

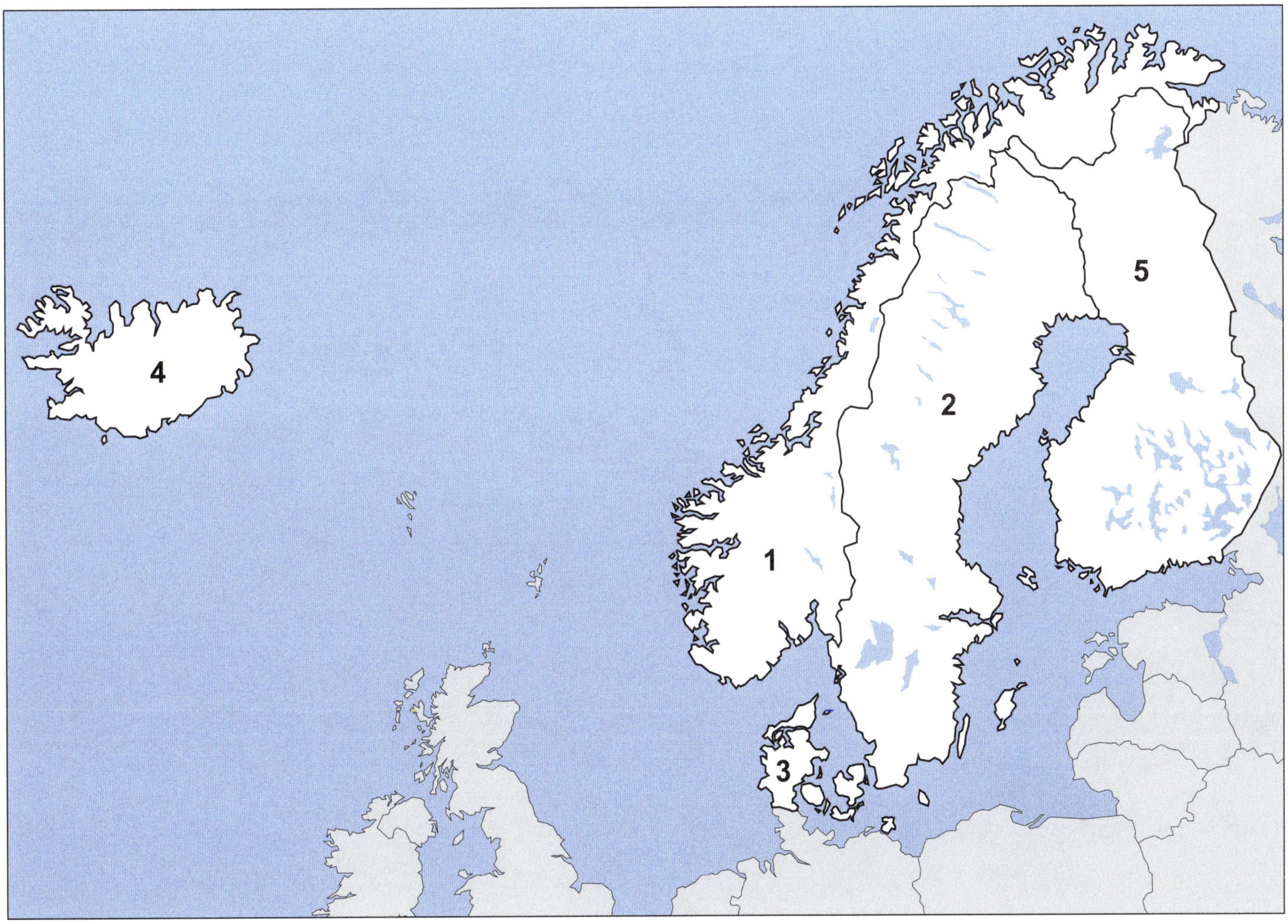

QUIZ 2

Eastern Europe: Part I

ANSWER KEY

Name:______________________________ Date:______________________

Score:______________

Use the map to fill out the blanks below. Remember to use correct spelling.

1. Country: Russia Capital: Moscow
2. Country: Estonia Capital: Tallinn
3. Country: Latvia Capital: Riga
4. Country: Lithuania Capital: Vilnius
5. Country: Belarus Capital: Minsk
6. Country: Ukraine Capital: Kyiv
7. Country: Poland Capital: Warsaw

QUIZ 3

Eastern Europe: Part II

ANSWER KEY

Name:______________________________ Date:____________________

Score:____________

Use the map to fill out the blanks below. Remember to use correct spelling.

1.	Country: Czech Republic	Capital: Prague
2.	Country: Slovakia	Capital: Bratislava
3.	Country: Hungary	Capital: Budapest
4.	Country: Romania	Capital: Bucharest
5.	Country: Moldova	Capital: Chisinau
6.	Country: Bulgaria	Capital: Sofia
7.	Country: Croatia	Capital: Zagreb
8.	Country: Bosnia & Herzegovina	Capital: Sarajevo
9.	Country: Montenegro	Capital: Podgorica
10.	Country: North Macedonia	Capital: Skopje
11.	Country: Kosovo	Capital: Pristina
12.	Country: Serbia	Capital: Belgrade
13.	Country: Slovenia	Capital: Ljubljana
14.	Country: Albania	Capital: Tirana

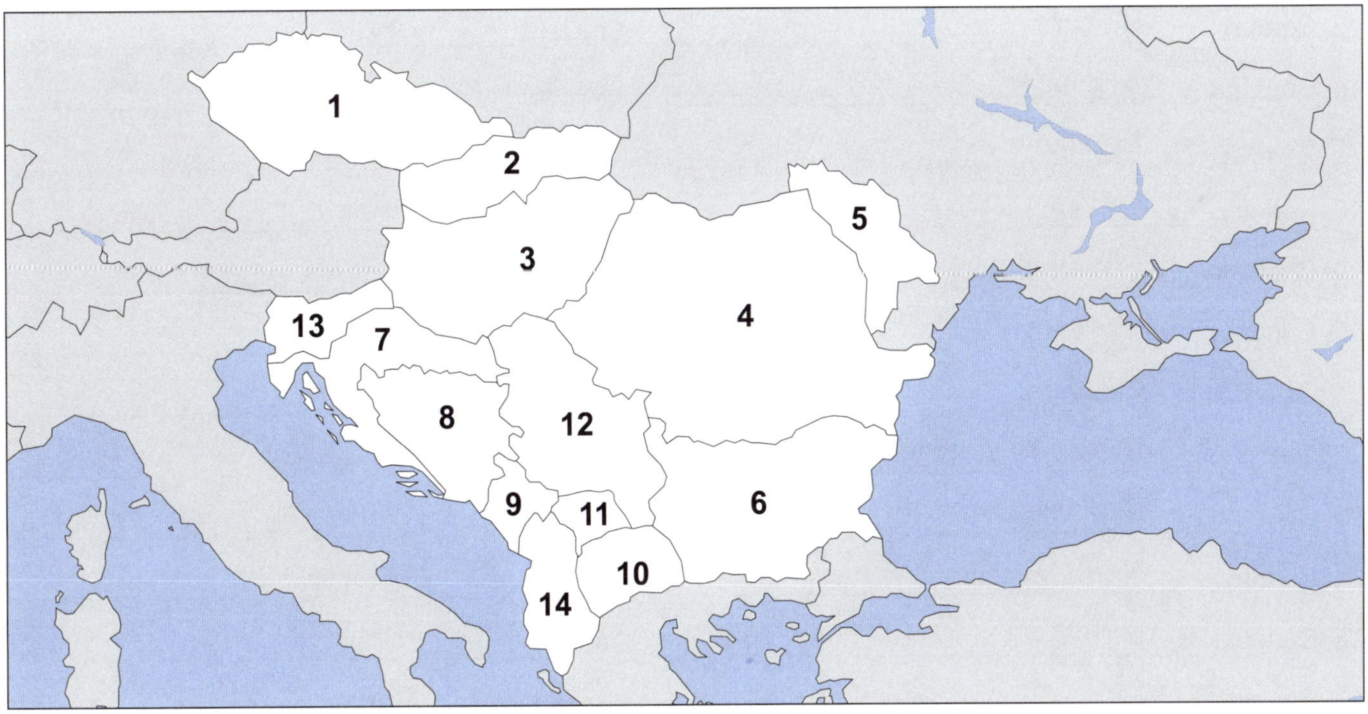

TEST

Europe: Part II

ANSWER KEY

Name:______________________________ Date:____________________

Score:____________

Use the map on the next page to fill out the blanks below. Remember to use correct spelling.

1. Country: Norway Capital: Oslo
2. Country: Sweden Capital: Stockholm
3. Country: Denmark Capital: Copenhagen
4. Country: Iceland Capital: Reykjavik
5. Country: Finland Capital: Helsinki
6. Country: Russia Capital: Moscow
7. Country: Belarus Capital: Minsk
8. Country: Ukraine Capital: Kyiv
9. Country: Poland Capital: Warsaw
10. Country: Czech Republic Capital: Prague
11. Country: Slovakia Capital: Bratislava
12. Country: Hungary Capital: Budapest
13. Country: Romania Capital: Bucharest
14. Country: Moldova Capital: Chisinau
15. Country: Bulgaria Capital: Sofia
16. Country: Albania Capital: Tirana
17. Country: Estonia Capital: Tallinn
18. Country: Latvia Capital: Riga
19. Country: Lithuania Capital: Vilnius
20. Country: Slovenia Capital: Ljubljana
21. Country: Croatia Capital: Zagreb
22. Country: Bosnia & Herzegovina Capital: Sarajevo
23. Country: Montenegro Capital: Podgorica
24. Country: North Macedonia Capital: Skopje
25. Country: Serbia Capital: Belgrade
26. Country: Kosovo Capital: Pristina

TEST

Europe: Part II

ANSWER KEY

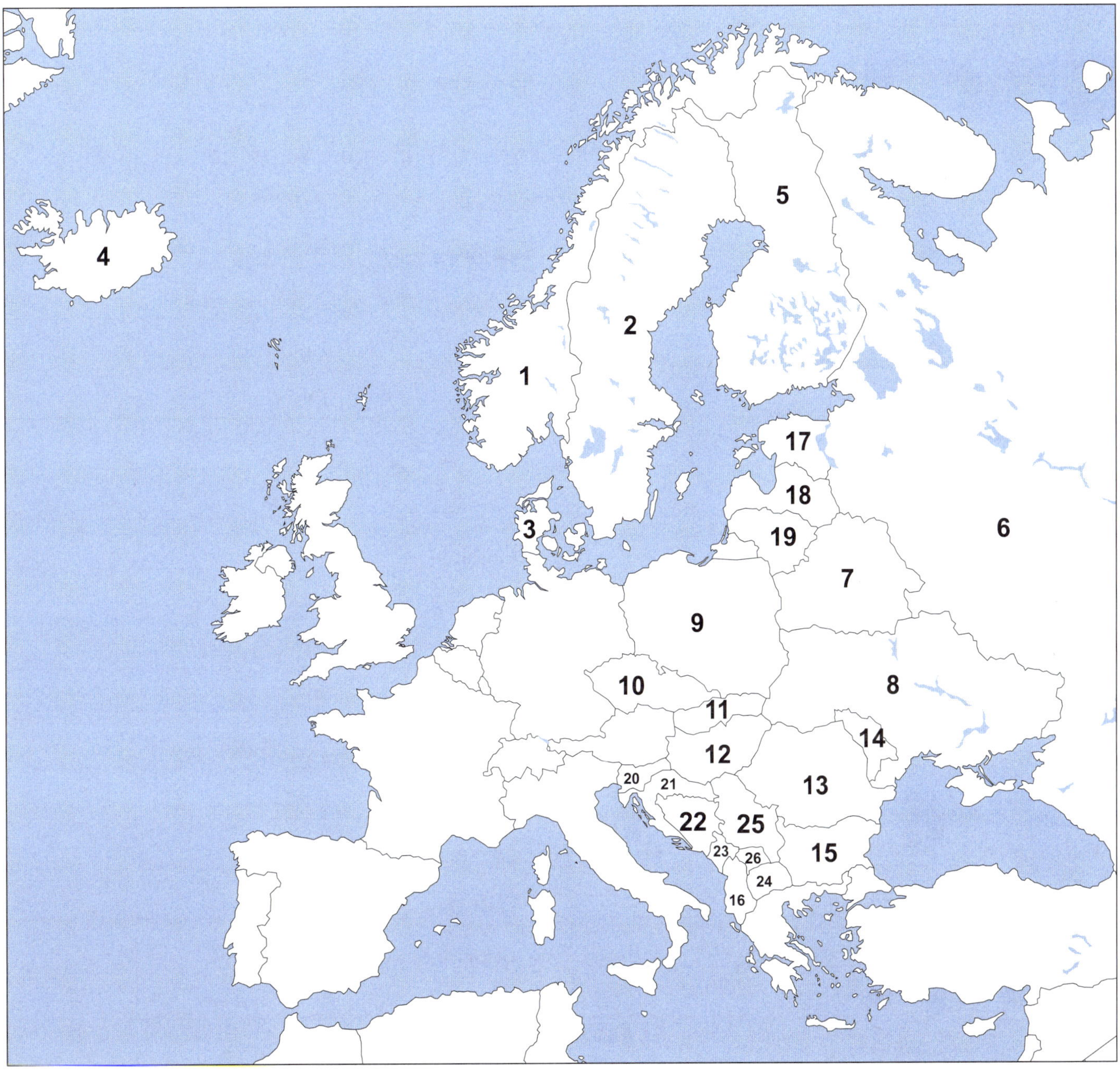

TEST

Europe

ANSWER KEY

Name:______________________________ Date:____________________

Score:__________

Use the map on the next page to fill out the blanks below. Remember to use correct spelling.

1. Country:	Greece	Capital:	Athens
2. Country:	Italy	Capital:	Rome
3. Country:	Spain	Capital:	Madrid
4. Country:	Portugal	Capital:	Lisbon
5. Country:	France	Capital:	Paris
6. Country:	Switzerland	Capital:	Bern
7. Country:	Liechtenstein	Capital:	Vaduz
8. Country:	Austria	Capital:	Vienna
9. Country:	Germany	Capital:	Berlin
10. Country:	Netherlands	Capital:	Amsterdam
11. Country:	Belgium	Capital:	Brussels
12. Country:	Luxembourg	Capital:	Luxembourg City
13. Country:	United Kingdom	Capital:	London
14. Country:	Ireland	Capital:	Dublin
15. Country:	Norway	Capital:	Oslo
16. Country:	Sweden	Capital:	Stockholm
17. Country:	Denmark	Capital:	Copenhagen
18. Country:	Iceland	Capital:	Reykjavik
19. Country:	Finland	Capital:	Helsinki
20. Country:	Russia	Capital:	Moscow
21. Country:	Belarus	Capital:	Minsk
22. Country:	Ukraine	Capital:	Kyiv
23. Country:	Poland	Capital:	Warsaw
24. Country:	Czech Republic	Capital:	Prague
25. Country:	Slovakia	Capital:	Bratislava

TEST

Europe

ANSWER KEY

26. Country: Hungary — Capital: Budapest
27. Country: Bulgaria — Capital: Sofia
28. Country: Moldova — Capital: Chisinau
29. Country: Romania — Capital: Bucharest
30. Country: Albania — Capital: Tirana
31. Country: Estonia — Capital: Tallinn
32. Country: Latvia — Capital: Riga
33. Country: Lithuania — Capital: Vilnius
34. Country: Slovenia — Capital: Ljubljana
35. Country: Croatia — Capital: Zagreb
36. Country: Bosnia & Herzegovina — Capital: Sarajevo
37. Country: Montenegro — Capital: Podgorica
38. Country: Serbia — Capital: Belgrade
39. Country: Kosovo — Capital: Pristina
40. Country: North Macedonia — Capital: Skopje

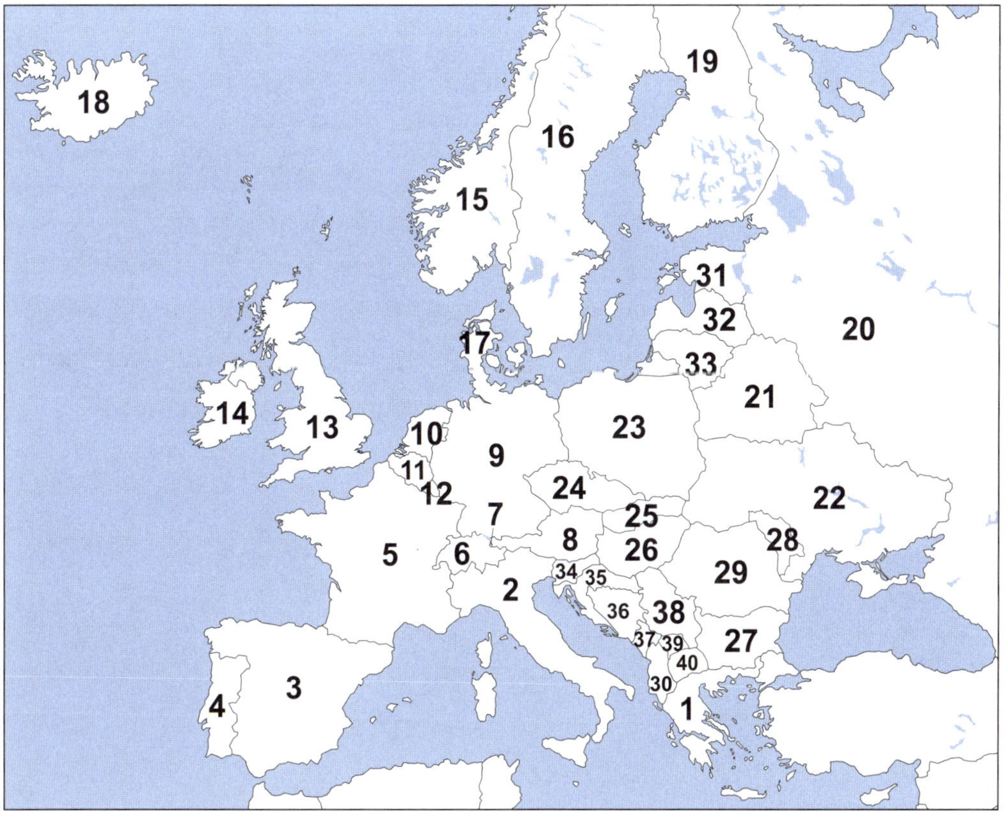

FINAL TEST

ANSWER KEY

Name:______________________________ Date:______________________

Score:______________

Use the map to place each country's number next to the name of the country and its capital.

4	Afghanistan	1	Ankara
3	Iran	3	Tehran
8	Iraq	4	Kabul
9	Israel	10	Islamabad
5	Jordan	2	Riyadh
7	Lebanon	5	Amman
10	Pakistan	9	Jerusalem
2	Saudi Arabia	7	Beirut
6	Syria	6	Damascus
1	Turkey	8	Baghdad

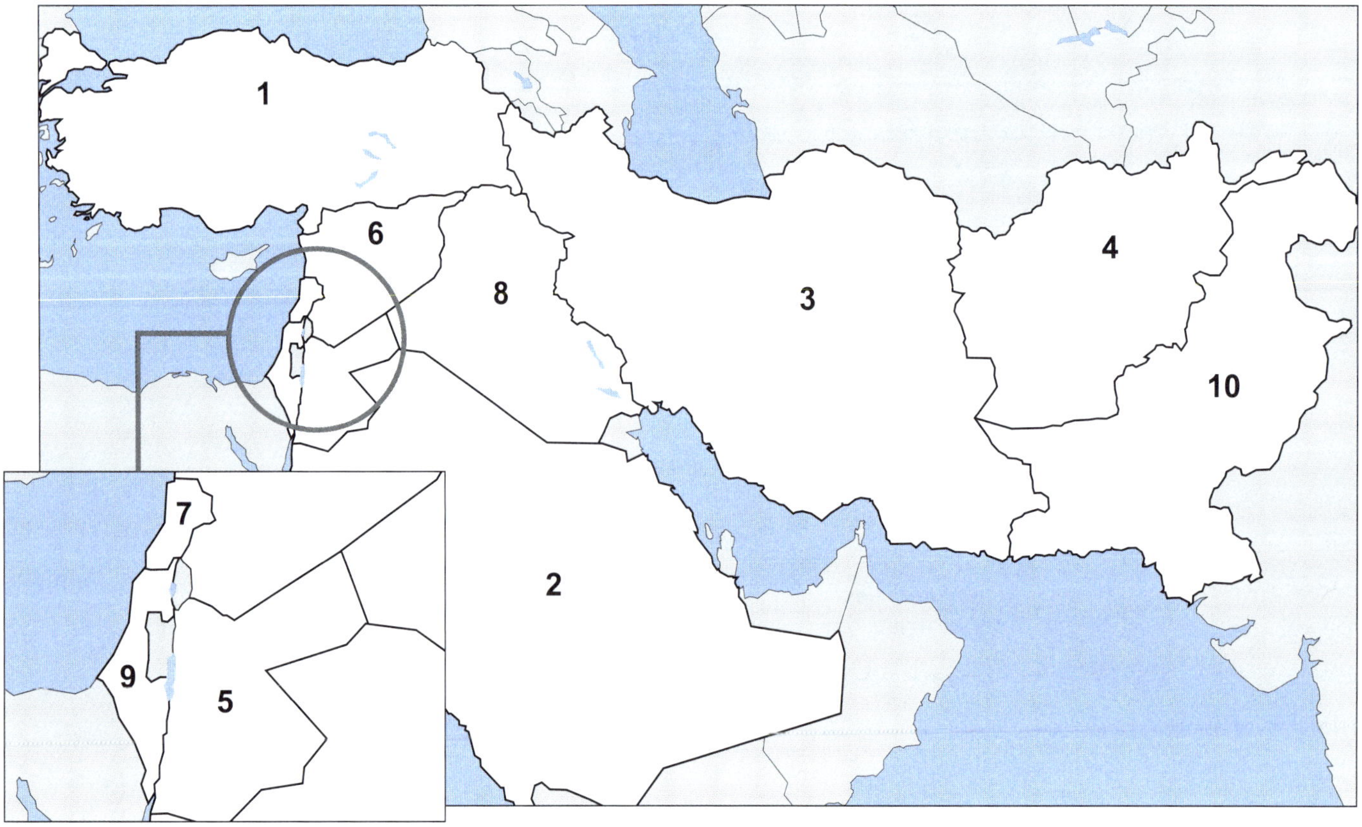

FINAL TEST

ANSWER KEY

Use the map to place each country's number next to the name of the country and its capital.

4	Algeria	6	Rabat
7	Egypt	4	Algiers
1	Libya	3	Tunis
6	Morocco	5	Juba
2	Sudan	1	Tripoli
3	Tunisia	7	Cairo
5	South Sudan	2	Khartoum

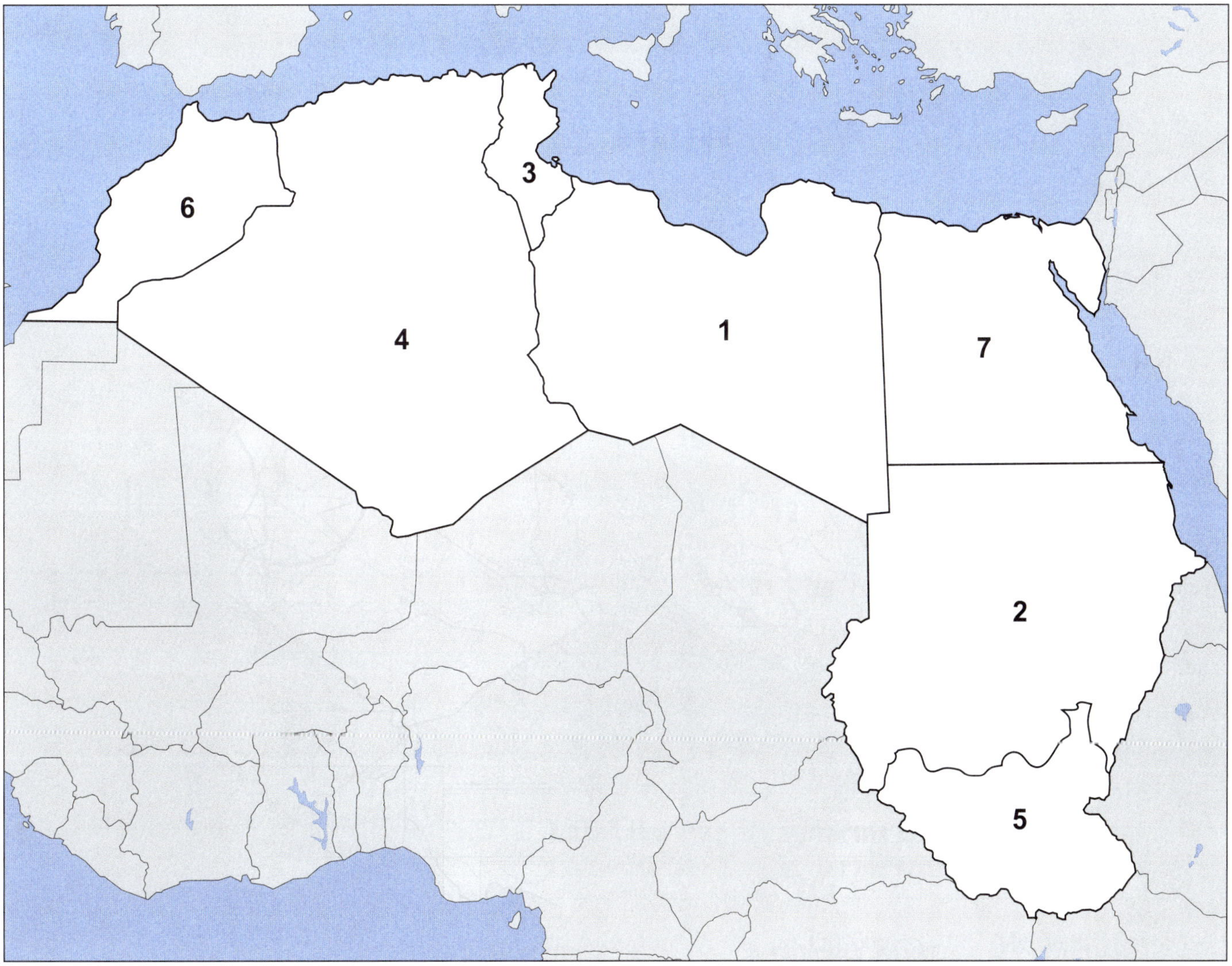

FINAL TEST

ANSWER KEY

Use the map to place each country's number next to the name of the country and its capital.

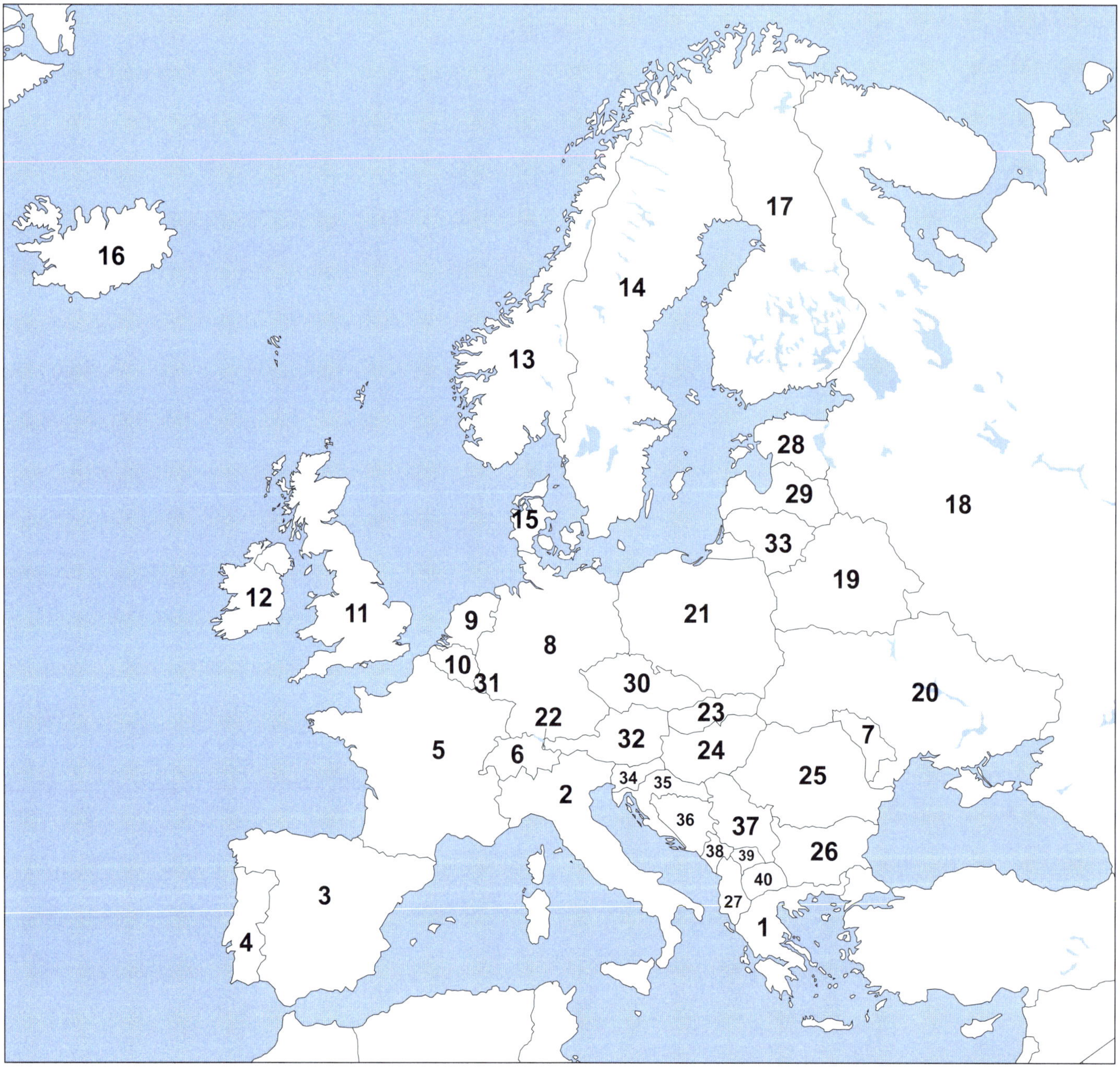

FINAL TEST

ANSWER KEY

COUNTRY

27	Albania	24	Hungary	21	Poland
32	Austria	16	Iceland	4	Portugal
19	Belarus	12	Ireland	25	Romania
10	Belgium	2	Italy	18	Russia
26	Bulgaria	39	Kosovo	37	Serbia
36	Bosnia & Herzegovina	29	Latvia	23	Slovakia
35	Croatia	22	Liechtenstein	34	Slovenia
30	Czech Republic	33	Lithuania	3	Spain
15	Denmark	31	Luxembourg	14	Sweden
28	Estonia	40	North Macedonia	6	Switzerland
17	Finland	7	Moldova	11	United Kingdom
5	France	38	Montenegro	20	Ukraine
8	Germany	9	Netherlands		
1	Greece	13	Norway		

CAPITAL

9	Amsterdam	20	Kyiv	16	Reykjavik
1	Athens	4	Lisbon	29	Riga
37	Belgrade	34	Ljubljana	2	Rome
8	Berlin	11	London	36	Sarajevo
6	Bern	31	Luxembourg City	40	Skopje
23	Bratislava	3	Madrid	26	Sofia
10	Brussels	19	Minsk	14	Stockholm
25	Bucharest	18	Moscow	28	Tallinn
24	Budapest	13	Oslo	27	Tirana
7	Chisinau	5	Paris	22	Vaduz
15	Copenhagen	38	Podgorica	32	Vienna
12	Dublin	30	Prague	33	Vilnius
17	Helsinki	39	Pristina	21	Warsaw
				35	Zagreb